FIGHTING THE SHADOW WARRIORS

A Marine in Vietnam

Harry Knickerbocker

For the walking dead.

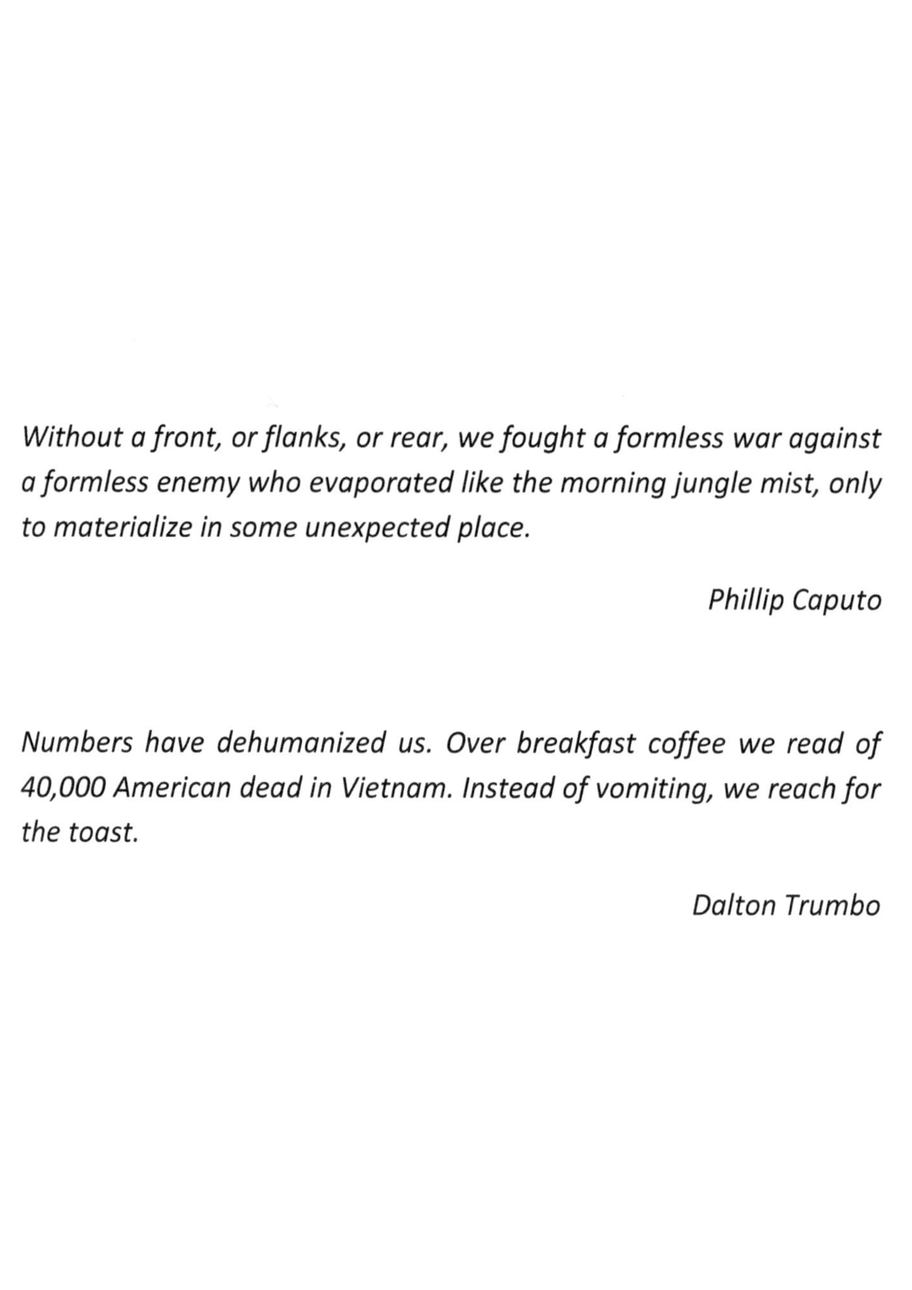

Without a front, or flanks, or rear, we fought a formless war against a formless enemy who evaporated like the morning jungle mist, only to materialize in some unexpected place.

Phillip Caputo

Numbers have dehumanized us. Over breakfast coffee we read of 40,000 American dead in Vietnam. Instead of vomiting, we reach for the toast.

Dalton Trumbo

Table of Contents

Not Home by Christmas

The water in the harbor at Danang was smooth and calm as we climbed down the Jacob's ladder into our Mike boats. All of our magazines were fully loaded. We also carried two full canteens, and our packs were stuffed full of C-rations and extra ammo. We carried our rifles slung over our shoulder. At the last minute, my squad leader gave each man in the squad two hand grenades.

"Expect to be shot at," he said. "It's going to be Ca hot landing. When the ramp goes down, get off the boat quickly. The gooks will be waiting for us on the beach. Pay attention. Get on line immediately, hit the deck, and begin returning fire. Don't bunch up, and follow my orders."

The date was June 16, 1965. After a long, boring voyage from Okinawa, my battalion had finally arrived in Vietnam. It was hot and muggy. Everyone was sweating profusely. I could smell the land from the deck of our troop transport. It was not a pleasant smell. It was earthy and repugnant. Vietnam smelled like fish, human feces, smoke from wood fires, and rotting vegetation.

My unit, Delta Company, 1st battalion, 9 Marines, was going ashore. We trained on Okinawa for a month and a half before we were given orders to proceed to Vietnam. We were so isolated with our training that we heard no news about the war. It didn't exist as far as we were concerned. Nobody was paying attention. We never talked about Vietnam. Our orders came as a surprise. As it turned out, we were going to guard the perimeter of the airbase at Danang. Operation Rolling Thunder was underway. Fighter bombers flew out of the airbase on a daily basis to bomb targets in North Vietnam. That made the airbase a first rate target for the VC. Our commanders needed an infantry unit to stand guard. We were the second Marine battalion to go ashore in Vietnam. Our arrival relieved the 3rd Battalion, 9th Marines. They were going home to the states. Their tour of duty was over. They spent about three months in Vietnam, and they had seen little or no action. Charlie was hard to find in those days.

After everyone was aboard the landing craft we left the ship. Then we got behind several other boats, and we began to circle around, and around. This went on for about a half hour. Because the water was so calm, nobody got seasick. Finally, someone issued a command. The Mike boats got on line, and then headed for the beach. We didn't know what to expect, so we naturally expected the worst. We thought we were going to make an amphibious landing in the proud tradition of those Marines who fought the Japanese. Our imaginations were working overtime. When you're inexperienced you're easy to deceive. The Mike boats chugged slowly toward the shore. There was no incoming fire. In fact, things were mildly boring. We had a slight tailwind that was blowing the diesel exhaust from the boat in our direction. It stank. My whole platoon had been jammed into the Mike boat. We stood shoulder to shoulder. We jostled into each other from time to time. And we patiently waited for the boat to hit the beach so the landing ramp would splash down and set us free.

I couldn't see over the boat's landing ramp. So I had no idea how far away from the shore we were. I was only aware of the other men in my platoon, and the movement of the boat. When we finally hit the beach I surged forward as the boat came to a stop. Then I braced myself. I prepared to exit the boat as quickly as possible. The most critical part of the landing was getting off of the boat. Men would bunch up as they ran down the landing ramp. They made easy targets.

We had to clear the ramp to get on line. I was all hyped up. I actually fixed my bayonet.

When the landing ramp splashed down, instead of hostile enemy fire, we ran ashore and were greeted by a crowd of unarmed Vietnamese, mostly women and children, who were selling Coca Cola...among other things. It was a strangely absurd situation. They had American products to sell and they were chasing the dollar. Capitalism was alive and doing well in Vietnam. They immediately crowded around us. Instead of spreading out, getting on line, and hitting the deck, we stood still and watched what was going on. It was unbelievable. It was also the first time I heard the Vietnamese language spoken. It sounded strange. It had a rhythm that was choppy, sharp, and irregular. Some of the Vietnamese had mastered a few words of English out of economic necessity.

"You buy Coca Cola?" One old woman asked. "Vely cheap. Vely good. One dollar twenty-five."

Before anyone in my squad could take her up on the offer, my squad leader, Corporal James intervened.

"Don't buy any Cokes," he said. "They may contain slivers of glass, or some kind of poison. You can't trust these people. Some of them may be VC sympathizers."

VC sympathizers? How could you tell? How could we separate the sympathizers from the non-sympathizers? Who could we trust? Steve Johnson was in my fire team. He was a close friend who always had something interesting to say.

"This is going to be a different kind of war," he said. "How are we going to separate the enemy from the civilians? How are we going to fight the VC without killing a lot of innocent people?"

I didn't have any good answers. He was right. This was going to be a different kind of war. It would be unlike any war the United States had ever fought. It would be so different that we never actually came up with a good strategy to win. All we ended up doing was counting dead bodies…ours and theirs. Then we created a mathematical ratio that was not unlike the slope of a right hand triangle's hypotenuse. In essence, the steeper the positive slope, the greater our victory…assuming the variable for our dead was on the x axis of a Cartesian graph. It was absolutely absurd. The ratio meant that we could only claim victory by degrees. A ratio of ten dead VC, for every American, was far more victorious than a ratio of two dead VC, for every American. And the same can be said for defeat. A ratio of one dead VC, for five Americans, was a more serious defeat than a ratio of one dead VC, for every two Americans. This transformed the war into something that resembled a parlor game. Under the influence of Secretary of Defense McNamara, our progress would be based on the statistics of death. And, as the war progressed, we discovered that we couldn't trust anyone but ourselves. We couldn't trust our own politicians, the American public, or the generals who were giving the orders. The war would ultimately be based on propaganda, delusions, and outright lies. From the very beginning the war was unwinnable.

But that was all in the future. On the day we landed in the harbor at Danang, nobody knew what we were getting into. Nobody knew how the war, years later, would go from bad to horrible. We were the new kids on the block. And we were Americans. We thought we were invincible. Our American idealism was a form of arrogance that was out of touch with reality. We thought we were better, smarter, and more courageous than the Vietnamese. We were absolutely certain that we would defeat the VC, and be home in time for Christmas. As things turned out, Vietnam was a country that had some terrible lessons to teach us about our pretentious feelings.

About a half hour after we came ashore we boarded some buses for the ride to the airbase. The windows of the buses were covered with wire mesh. I assumed that the mesh was supposed to protect us from hand grenades being tossed into the bus. Our route to the airbase went through the center of the city. As I glanced out of the window, I looked at the crowds gathered around open air stalls that were selling various goods. I felt out of place. I was a western white guy. The people in the streets were Asians. They dressed differently. They spoke a different language. I began to wonder what was going to happen. My future was highly uncertain. Fear crept into my gut and made me nervous. I was a complete stranger, in a strange land. I'd come to fight a strange war, with a strange, illusive enemy. It was going to take some time to adjust to my new surroundings.

The buses dropped us off at the airbase. Then we walked about a quarter of a mile to a series of tents. This was our new home for the next several weeks as we acclimated to the overbearing heat and humidity. We moved in and tried to relax. Early the next day we were assigned guard posts on the western perimeter of the airbase. Just beyond my position was a high fence that bordered a minefield that was about fifty feet deep. Its limit was marked by an outer fence. Beyond the fence was a village that we began to call Dog Patch. It consisted of half a dozen run down houses, several dirt roads, and a few palm trees. Standing watch was boring in the extreme. The hours seemed to creep by on broken legs. Spying on the civilians as they went about their business in Dog Patch offered some relief. There was nothing else to do. The sun came up, and the sun went down.

After our period of acclimation was over, we left the airbase behind. We moved out into the country and established our first company perimeter. Then we began to go on patrols. We were actively looking to engage Charlie. But he wasn't playing our game. He was nowhere to be found. We were in greater danger of dying from friendly fire, than by the hand of our enemy. Because we were new to the war, some of our guys were prone to being trigger happy. There was also the danger of accidental discharges. In fact, a black guy named Leroy was accidently shot by a white guy named Alex. Leroy stood on the edge of their foxhole. Alex was standing in the bottom. He aimed his rifle up at Leroy. He was just screwing around. Leroy grabbed the rifle by the muzzle to push it away. The rifle went off and shot him in the stomach. It was a terrible mistake. Luckily, Leroy survived. But he spent months in a VA hospital. As new guys, we were our own worst enemy. Our inexperience was dangerous.

I don't know if we brought the war to the country, or the country brought the war to us. Maybe it was some of both. As time passed, we gradually became more and more a part of the landscape. And we eventually discovered how our shadowy enemy operated. We started taking a few casualties from booby-traps, and anti-personnel mines. We found out the hard way that every village we entered was a potential death trap. There was no shortage of punji pits with sharp bamboo stakes. And trip wires connected to booby traps could kill you in a heartbeat. We discovered just how brutally inventive the VC actually were. Charlie was a smart, clever, and very determined enemy. As the war progressed, I think many of us began to realize that we had underestimated him. We also began to realize that Charlie was in it for the long haul. There wasn't going to be any quick or easy victory. And, in spite of our hopeful thoughts to the contrary, this meant that we would not be going home by Christmas.

Tossing Peebles

I never knew where we were going when we were ordered to climb on board the choppers. If someone had given me a map to look at it would have been entirely pointless. I could never have placed the tip of my index finger on our next destination. We could have been headed anywhere. We were always lost. All we knew for sure was the immediate ground under our muddy boots.

I followed the other men in my squad. I always followed the other men in my squad. There was strength in numbers. Vietnam was not a good place to be alone…unless you had a death wish. So I located myself relative to the positions of the other men in my squad. This was the best I could do. And only the immediate lay of the land made sense. Staying alive meant using the earth, every rise and fall, every tree line, every hill, every valley, every stream, and every rice paddy dike.

I was the first fire team leader. The guys called me Nickolas. There were only ten men in my squad… including the squad leader. We had three fire teams composed of three men. We were operating at reduced strength. Normally there were thirteen men in a squad. We had taken some casualties in our platoon. Our unit went on one operation after another. We climbed into the choppers, and then flew off. After we landed in an LZ, we created a temporary defense perimeter. After the whole platoon had arrived, we formed a column and headed into the nearby jungle. Or, we walked off into rice paddies dotted by small primitive villages that were loaded with booby traps.

I hated Vietnam. I was afraid I would die before my tour of duty was over. In fact, I was certain I would die. I thought I would be shot through the head and then fall face first into the muddy brown water of a rice paddy. And if the bullet didn't kill me, I would suck putrid water into my lungs and drown. This is what I imagined. It was a waking nightmare that haunted me from one day to the next. My death seemed to be unavoidable. Vietnam was a country dominated by death and destruction. It was a country you could easily die in. You could be walking slowly down a trail, paying close attention, doing everything right, and a booby trap would blow off your arms and legs. Just walking was a mortal threat. Every time you put your foot down you took a risk. You could be wading across a rice paddy and a sniper's bullet would hit you in the chest. An enemy mortar round could turn your body into a bloody mass of lifeless meat. You could step into a punji pit full of sharpened bamboo stakes and die from septicemia. The VC coated the tips of the stakes with human shit. The VC were very inventive. They could turn a C-ration can into a lethal weapon. So…I thought I would surely die. I thought it was just a matter of time. I thought my days were numbered.

And there was nothing glorious about dying in Vietnam. There was no Hollywood heroism, and no famous last words. Mister Death didn't give a shit about phony drama. He could show up anytime of the day or night and take you away. Living or dying was mostly about luck. Our training as Marines had limits. No matter how much training you received, the reality of combat came as a terrible shock. And Mister Death didn't care about who you were. He didn't care about your personality, your rank, your race, your religion, your politics, your age, or whether or not you were smart or dumb. Mister Death is blind. He doesn't take names or look at faces. He's very impersonal. He doesn't care who you are. And he has a big blank space on his chest where the word mercy should have been written.

The war was a cold green machine that ran on fear, anger, and hatred...especially hatred. I hated the heat, rain, mosquitoes, leeches, rice paddies, jungle, fire fights, booby traps, jungle rot, rear echelon motherfuckers, and C-rations. But most of all I hated the VC…and the villagers that supported them. War is a brutal lesson in adversity. If you weren't tough mentally and physically, you'd break down and go insane. I knew guys who couldn't take the firefights. Their knees would shake so bad they couldn't stand up and move forward. They'd curl up in the fetal position behind the nearest rice paddy dike. They'd refuse to aim their rifles. They were worthless. And they were transferred out of our company.

We were tough. We were tough because the war made us tough. We were trained to kill. And the Marines are among the very best when it comes to killing their enemy. Many of my friends seemed to enjoy it. At least they acted as if they enjoyed it. It was all just part of being a tough guy, in a tough war, with a tough, very determined enemy. Trying to be kind and compassionate would turn you into a pussy in the eyes of your fellow Marines. There was no room for guys who were soft. We had to be ready for anything. We trusted each other with our lives.

One hot afternoon my squad leader ordered us to saddle up. He was a twenty-one year old corporal from New York named Richard James. He'd been my squad leader for over a year.

"There's a Huey gunship that's been shot down south of the airbase," Corporal James said loudly. "It's taking enemy fire. They want us to rescue the crew. So get your shit together. Our choppers will be here in a few minutes. Move it! Every second counts! It's gonna be a hot LZ!"

In less than ten minutes we were outbound on choppers for some LZ that was south of the airbase at Danang. We sat in silence. The chopper's motor was too loud to talk. The chopper shook and vibrated. We flashed the idiot grin at each other. We held on. We were excited. Adrenalin made everyone hyperactive. Several of the guys in my fire team took off their helmets and sat on them to protect their ass from bullets. It was a joke. A helmet will not stop a bullet. We expected to be shot at after we went into the death spiral that preceded our landing. Instead of coming straight into the LZ, the pilots would put their chopper into a spiral that circled down to a fast landing, and an equally fast discharge of the Marines on board. This was something we had done numerous times. We knew the drill upside down and backwards. I spotted the downed gunship as we approached the LZ. It was lying on its right side. Its rotors had been broken off and its tail was broken and bent. Presumably, the crew was rescued just after their gunship went down.

A minute later we jumped off and ran to establish a defense perimeter. It was a circle with the gunship in its center. My fire team ended up in a section that faced outward toward flat sandy ground. There was no rice paddy. There was nothing but low scrubby weeds and sand for hundreds of yards. It was a good position. We also discovered that the guys in some prior unit had dug a number of foxholes. They were situated in exactly the right place so we jumped in. The holes were about ten yards apart. We had a terrific view. We leaned back and relaxed. There was no enemy fire. Our landing had been unopposed.

The guys in my fire team sat in their foxholes and waited for the recovery team to do their job. We were bored. The sun was high overhead and very hot. I could feel my head cooking in sweat. Then I felt a light ping on my helmet. When I turned to look I could see that Steve was tossing small pebbles at me. He was laughing. I searched the bottom of my foxhole, found a few pebbles, and then I returned fire. We were bored and having fun. Steve was crazy. He was always up to something. I think his constant joking around was a way of dealing with our steady supply of chaos and bullshit.

Our perimeter had a diameter of about a hundred meters. My fire team was in the northern section. The southern section faced a tree line that was about two hundred meters away from our perimeter. And behind the tree line was a small village. I could only see three structures. They didn't look like homes. They looked more like storage sheds. While Steve and I were tossing pebbles back and forth, a squad patrol was sent into the village to check things out. Along the way they came to a creek they had to wade across. It was not very deep. It was easy going. After searching the village they didn't find anything interesting. A few minutes later they began their return. When they came to the creek they decided to cross back over in a different spot. The squad leader was a good friend of mine. His name was Johnny MacDowell. He was a sergeant on his second enlistment. He was also short. He stood about five feet seven. He was wearing a fully loaded pack that weighed thirty or forty pounds. He was carrying his rifle at port arms. He was walking point. When he waded into the creek he suddenly sank under the water. The creek was much deeper in the new spot. He couldn't rise to the surface because of his heavy pack and rifle. Luckily, the guy behind him was over six feet tall. When he saw Johnny's helmet bobbing around he quickly pulled him to safety. When I talked with him, after we returned to our platoon perimeter that evening, he was still rattled.

"I goddamn near drowned," he exclaimed. "If Evan hadn't grabbed me I would have died. What a shitty way to go. This country can kiss my ass. It's not worth saving. It's not worth the life of a single fucking Marine."

The afternoon was quietly passing by. The guys from the air wing were getting the downed gunship ready to be hauled out. They had to hook up a cradle of supporting cables. In the meantime we held our perimeter. Everyone stayed down behind cover. We had three M60 machine guns in our platoon and they were all pointed at the distant tree line. Our platoon commander, Second Lieutenant Ralph Dawson, was sure that if we received small arms fire it would come from the tree line. So he placed the machineguns to take care of the problem. And he was right.

The first enemy shots rang out just as a huge chopper approached the LZ and went into a hover over the damaged gunship. The noise from the chopper was so loud we could barely hear the VC small arms fire. They were shooting at the big chopper, trying to bring it down. The reaction was instantaneous. Everyone on the southern side of the perimeter opened fire. From my fire team's position, on the northern side of our perimeter, there was nothing to be done. So we just sat in our foxholes and watched the show. The big chopper quickly gave up the rescue attempt and flew away.

The firefight went on and on. There was probably five or six VC who were taking on a platoon of Marines. They would take a few shots and then duck down for cover. And then, when our small arms fire slacked off, they would pop up again and take a few more shots. There were no casualties on our side. The fight went on for about twenty minutes. Then Marine close air support suddenly arrived. There were two A4 that seemed to materialize out of nowhere. The pilots knew exactly what they were doing. They aimed at the tree line. On their first pass they covered the target with twenty millimeter cannon fire. I was very impressed. There was a lightning fast series of explosions that literally tore down the trees. Leaves, twigs, and limbs flew off in every direction. I was sure the VC had been killed. But I was wrong. Just after the second A4 made its pass, the VC popped back up and fired a few more shots at us. On the next pass the two A4 fired some rockets. There were more explosions, and more destruction to the tree line. But the VC were unfazed. They continued to shoot at us. On the next pass bombs were dropped. But they were also ineffective. I was incredulous. What tremendous bravery on the part of the VC. Clearly, they believed in their cause. They were willing to die for it. Was I willing to die for my cause? Did I even have a cause? I didn't think so. In fact, at that point in time my only cause was to keep me and my buddies alive. I didn't give a shit about winning the fucking war. I didn't give a shit about defending the Constitution, democracy, our paranoid government, or even my fellow Americans. I just wanted to stay alive. I wanted to survive the war so I could go home, find a beautiful girlfriend, and give her a big kiss.

On their final pass the A4 dropped two napalm canisters. I watched them tumble down through the blue sky. A moment later the entire tree line erupted in a swirling cloud of fire and dense black smoke. It looked like hell on earth. As the fire burned down we waited to see if the VC were still alive. We waited to see if they were going to take a few more shots. Maybe they were able to run away. Or maybe they were still sitting in their spider holes when the napalm exploded. Either way, the fire fight was over. The guys on the firing line began to stand up. The big chopper flew back in, hooked up with the damaged gunship, and carried it away. A half hour later our own choppers landed. We climbed aboard and flew back to our regular platoon perimeter.

As I thought things over I began to suspect that we were not going to win the war. Our enemy not only lived in the neighborhood, they were willing to take greater risks. I thought our enemy was more courageous than us. They were willing to die for their country.

A Trash Can Full Of Garbage

We were up and assembled before the crack of dawn. In the dark I could see a line of amphibious amtracks. They were sitting in a convoy with their diesel engines running. I could smell their exhaust smoke. Their drivers waited while we climbed aboard. Everybody decided to ride on top rather than inside. We wanted to see what was going on. We'd been told by our squad leader, Corporal James that we were going to head up a nearby river. After we reached our objective, a village named Cam Ne, we'd do a left flanking movement, come out of the river on line, and then, after the amtracks came to a halt, we would jump off, and form a skirmish line that faced the village. That was the plan.

I knew very little about the village of Cam Ne. Scuttlebutt said that when Marines had swept through the village on prior occasions they had been shot at by snipers. They had also taken a few casualties from booby traps. This being the case, Cam Ne was judged to be an enemy village. I thought we'd just sweep through the village, search for VC suspects, and then we'd leave. We'd climb back aboard the amtracks, go back down the river, and then we'd return to the sandbagged bunkers on our company perimeter. Then we'd drink a cup of C-ration coffee, eat some ham and motherfuckers, and forget all about Cam Ne. It was just another operation.

The river was calm and muddy. It was also shallow in some places. The amtrack to our immediate front actually got stuck. Its tracks couldn't get a grip on the muddy bottom, and there wasn't enough water to float it free. So it came to a stop. This delayed our progress. It took about a half hour for another amtrack to pull the one that was stuck back into deep water. Our convoy then continued.

As we sat on top of the amtrack we watched the shore line slowly pass by. The amtrack was only going five or six miles an hour. In the morning half-light we checked out the passing line of bushes and trees on the nearby shore. We were looking for the telltale silhouettes of VC snipers. There wasn't much talking going on. We never talked much when we were in Indian Territory. You had to pay close attention. You had to keep your mouth shut and your eyes open. Riding on top of the amtrack, in full view, turned us into easy targets.

But my buddy Steve just couldn't keep quiet. He knew we were vulnerable, and he was nervous. So he had to say something.

"Quack, quack, quack," he said quietly. "I feel like a sitting duck. If we get shot at we'll have to jump in the fucking river for cover."

"You always look on the bright side of things," Jason Newsom said. He was another member of my fire team. "Try to think positive thoughts for once."

"Positive thoughts?" Steve asked. "Are you fucking kidding? In Vietnam? I'm afraid all of my positive thoughts have vanished. They left my brain the day I arrived in this shitty country. They didn't want anything do with this crazy fucking war. They went and got jobs working for the Peace Corp."

Several hours after the convoy began its journey we finally arrived at the village of Cam Ne. It was around seven in the morning. The convoy of amtracks all turned ninety degrees to the left at the same time. Then they moved out of the river on line, and came to rest about a hundred feet from the village. We jumped off, spread out, and formed a wide skirmish line. Then we hit the deck with our rifles pointed at the village. We were lying in a dry, sandy rice paddy. My squad was on the far left flank of the line. I think most of the people in the village were still asleep, or just getting up, when we made our initial approach. We lay still and waited for the order to move into the village. The amtracks had turned off their engines. It was unusually quiet. There were no dogs barking, birds singing, or children laughing and playing.

Then some VC snipers decided to do their duty. A series of rifle shots shattered the morning calm. I don't know how many snipers there were…maybe two or three? In any event, we returned fire. The whole skirmish line exploded. But it was a stupid reaction because nobody knew what they were shooting at. I knew the snipers had caught a hat immediately after they opened fire. That was their usual trick. They were long gone. So there were no visible targets. But that didn't matter at all. Guys just fired their rifles straight into the village. It was a case of pray and spray. Only innocent people remained in the village. And they were men who were too old and worn out to be VC, women who were both young and old, and children. All of the healthy young men in the village would be gone. They were either outright members of a VC unit, or they were afraid we would take them away as VC suspects. After ten or so seconds of heavy rifle fire our company gunny called for us to cease fire. The two or three snipers were lousy shots. They didn't hit anyone. However, a platoon sergeant was shot in the leg by one of his own Marines. The sergeant was out in front of our line when the shooting started. It was a dumb move on his part. He was our only casualty. Then the order came down to move into the village. So we got up and walked forward on line. We carried our rifles braced on our hips with the muzzles pointed forward. There was no more sniper fire. As soon as we entered the village, the order came down the line to torch the homes of the Vietnamese. I don't know who gave the order. I don't know if the order came from division, regiment, battalion, or from our own company commander: Captain Robert Gray. But whoever gave that order, was not a Marine. He was a fucking Nazi.

I joined the Marines at the age of seventeen. I joined because I wanted to stand in the shadow of the Marines who fought so bravely in the war against the Japanese. Those Pacific Island campaigns were almost mythical. And the Marines that fought them were great heroes. I admired and respected their service to the country. And I wanted to follow along in their footsteps.

What I saw in the village of Cam Ne disgraced the Marine Corps. We stopped being Marines walking on the right side of history. We turned into thugs. We turned into school yard bullies. We were no more different than the Nazis when they burned down countless villages on their way to take Moscow.

My fire team was located on the far left flank of the skirmish line so we had nothing to do but move slowly forward. On our immediate left was a wide open rice paddy. So we often stood around smoking and talking while other Marines in my unit pulled out their Zippo cigarette lighters and torched the thatched roofs of home after home. We watched women wailing and crying. We saw children clinging to their mothers in fear. We saw old men shaking their fist at the Marines. The bamboo posts that supported the homes exploded like pistol shots. The air was filled with smoke and flame. Spiders, centipedes, cockroaches, and mice, vacated the thatch of the burning roofs. They skittered and crawled down to the edge and jumped onto the ground. Then they ran into the bushes. There was nothing the villagers could do to stop the lunacy. They were completely helpless. Their faces were filled with anger and fear. They were at our mercy. Some of them begged and pleaded for us to spare their homes. But they were speaking in Vietnamese, and no one paid any attention to them. We were treating these Vietnamese as if they were a sub-species of the human race.

I was ashamed to be a Marine. The feeling was new. It undermined my pride and twisted my sense of right and wrong. I wanted to turn away, to not see what was taking place, to somehow resist the inhumanity. What was the fucking point? Why were we punishing these people? They were victims of the conflict. They posed no threat to us. We turned them into enemies for no good reason. We were destroying their village because several incompetent snipers had taken a few shots at us? What a lousy excuse. Our actions were crazy and self-defeating.

Morley Safer, and a CBS film crew, accompanied us on the operation. Mister Safer faithfully filmed the events of that day for the evening news. And not long after the sweep was over, his coverage made the air waves. It shocked the American public and cast a bad light on the Marines. We were not behaving as our forebears had behaved. We were not brave and courageous. We were running amok. We turned into animals. When we put on our war face we took off our humanity and hung it on a nearby clothes hook. In a guerilla war that's a really stupid thing to do. You can't fight the war without the support of the indigenous population. And you'll never get their support by burning down their homes…or killing them in a haphazard fusillade of rifle fire. A ten year old boy was collateral damage. He had been shot through the head.

Steve was watching everything that was taking place. He was chain smoking cigarettes.

"You know Nickolas," he said quietly, "this fucking war is turning my mind into a trash can full of garbage."

I knew what he meant. Everything we saw shocked our conscience, poisoned our memories, and degraded the value of life. The war was turning into a curse. I knew we would be haunted by our memories for years to come. There was just nothing good going on. Everything was bad. It was evil. My young delusions about heroism, and glory, had run into a brick wall. Cam Ne was unreal. It was a waking nightmare. What were we doing?

Time Magazine said we burned one hundred and fifty homes to the ground. I guess someone had flown over the village and made an official count. For our part, when the last home had gone up in flames, we returned to our Amtrack, climbed back on top, and then we headed back down the river for our home base. Our job was done.

"I thought we were supposed to be protecting these people from communist tyranny," Jason said angrily. "Shit! We ain't protecting no one. Those poor fucking people need to be protected from us. Forget the fucking communists."

"It was an enemy village," Corporal James said. "It had to be destroyed."

"Those people didn't look like enemies to me," Steve said. "They looked to me like people caught up in a war they have no control over. They have to say yes to whoever has the guns."

"The Marine Corps said it was an enemy village," Corporal James said again. "And we have to follow orders. We don't have a choice."

"I think we are creating our enemy," I said. "I think we are stereotyping these people, and turning them into targets."

"It was an enemy village," Corporal James said for a third time. "And we have to destroy our enemies…or they'll destroy us. There's no room for a soft heart."

"I think what we did is immoral," Jason said.

"Immoral?" Corporal James said. I could see that he was getting angry. "You've got to be shitting me. Every fucking war that's ever been fought was immoral. There are no good wars. And in the end, after the politicians who send young men to fight and die wash their hands and walk away, after all the generals retire, and the public forgets about all the killing, the guys that fought the war will end up sitting in a room all alone with their bad memories. We are going to be left holding the fucking bag. That's the way it's always been. The guys that do the fighting always pay the price."

In the aftermath, our company commander, Captain Gray, was relieved. And Gunny Hitchens was sent to another rifle company. He'd been the one that was yelling orders to burn the place down. For several hours I could hear him shouting above the pop of burning bamboo, and the roar of the flames. He was doing his job with gusto. He was following orders. I don't know if Cam Ne was the first village that the US military burned to the ground, but it certainly wasn't the last. Before the war was over thousands of villages would be judged as enemy strongholds, and then put to flames using cigarette lighters. Scorched earth became the norm. In essence, we ended up destroying the very people we were supposed to be saving. We couldn't tell who was a VC soldier, and who was an ordinary rice farmer. So, over time, we began to treat every villager as an enemy. We thought that making distinctions was a dangerous thing to do. Our paranoia was out of control.

Another Hot Day

It was around nine o'clock at night. My platoon was gathered together to watch the movie El Cid, with Sophia Loren, and Charlton Heston. We used a bed sheet for a screen. How someone was able to come up with a bed sheet was a big mystery. We were entranced by Sophia Loren's beauty, her marvelous face and body, her deep dark eyes, her lovely cheekbones, and her sensuous lips. We thought Charlton Heston was the luckiest man in the world. He got to play love scenes with Sophia Loren. We hadn't seen a movie in months so we were really enjoying the show.

Our company was sitting in a defensive perimeter several miles west of the airbase at Danang. We were just north of hill 327. We could see the airbase back down the valley. We were in a quiet location. There was no sniper fire. And the village, just across a rice paddy from our position, seemed to be safe. Day after long day we sat in our foxholes and surveyed the area to our direct front. It was boring in the extreme. At night we stood fifty percent watch. This meant there was one guy awake, and one guy asleep in each foxhole. Our only enemy was mosquitoes. They came out in the evening and were absolutely ravenous. They swarmed around and stung us without mercy. We put on insect repellent to keep them away but it wasn't that effective. When we slept we rolled up tight in our ponchos. But there was always one adventurous mosquito who managed to find a way in. You could hear it buzzing around looking for some exposed skin to stab with its needle-like nose.

The movie got to the scene where El Cid kills Sophia Loren's father after a prolonged fight. While her father is lying on his back in the dirt of an arena, El Cid runs him through with a sword. From that point on Sophia Loren hates El Cid. But everyone knows that she actually loves him, and that they will eventually work everything out. But we didn't get to see that part of the movie.

Our company gunny was a real prick. He was short, loud, and bad tempered. He also had a big nose, and big feet. He was a lifer who had served in Korea where he won a Bronze Star. His name was John Mathews. At one point in time, when he was a staff sergeant, he had been my platoon commander. Then he was promoted to gunnery sergeant, and he became our company gunny. He was also a terrific kiss ass. He played the tough guy to impress our company commander, Captain David Lawrence. He would boss us around and treat us like we were idiots just to show that he was in charge.

And just after El Cid killed Sophia Loren's father in the movie, Gunny Mathews began to yell for us to shut off the fucking projector. Then he walked over and angrily tore down the bed sheet. He wanted us to go back to our foxholes. He was a real spoil sport. As a result, I had no idea how the movie turned out. Years would pass before I was able to see the movie from beginning to end.

After we returned to our foxholes we set the watch and prepared ourselves for another long night. I didn't think anything was going to happen. But I was wrong. And Gunny Mathews was right to shut down the movie. Around eleven o'clock the big airbase at Danang came under attack by a large group of VC sappers. They were armed with satchel charges and hand grenades. They were backed up by several four deuce mortars which made a hell of a bang when they went off. The general plan for the VC attack was simple. The sappers entered through the south end of the airbase, which, believe it or not, had been left unguarded. Then they ran down the flight line and tried to destroy as many airplanes and choppers as they could. I heard one explosion after another. In a short period of time I saw fires burning in the clear night air. There was also a lot of shooting. The sky was filled with red tracers. The Marines in the air wing were defending the flight line. There was a real battle going on. And it wasn't that far away. It was exciting! Adrenalin raced through my blood!

Then I heard Gunny Mathews yell for us to saddle up. We were going to climb onto a convoy of trucks that were already on the way to pick us up. Once we were onboard, we were going to head down the valley to join the fight. So, we quickly grabbed our rifles, and put on our packs. As things turned out, we never came back to that quiet valley. We were on a one way trip.

The truck drivers put the pedal to the metal and we flew down the dirt road that led to the airbase in record time. It was a rough road so everybody hung on tight and tried not to bounce around. It didn't take long for us to reach the gate at the north end of the field. After we passed through, the lead driver aimed for the main runway that ran north and south. Then he sped toward the southern end of the strip. All the trucks behind him just followed along and matched his manic pace. When we came to the end of the runway everybody jumped out, got on line, and then lay down on the ground with their rifles pointed south. There was absolutely no cover. The land was flat and wide open. It was covered by scrubby low lying weeds. About a hundred feet away was a mesh fence that ran east to west. We didn't know that the sappers had come through that fence to make their attack. We didn't know much of anything really. And by the time we arrived the attack was over and the damage was done. Four or five aircraft had been destroyed. Around twenty or so sappers had been shot and killed by Marines in the air wing, or by rear echelon motherfuckers. The sappers had been on a suicide mission. I'm not at all sure the cost they paid in blood was worth the benefit. Anyway, there was nothing left for us to do. So we just lay on our bellies with our rifles pointed toward the mesh fence. And that's how we spent the rest of the night. There were no more sappers to kill.

In the early morning we boarded choppers and were soon outbound for an LZ somewhere south of the airbase. We were supposed to go looking for the four deuce mortars that had been used by the VC in their attack the night before. Four deuce mortars are big and heavy. They are sometimes mounted on small wheels, and they are not easy to transport. Someone in our high command believed there was a good chance the VC had buried the mortars after the attack, or hid them in some nearby hooch. As a result, we were ordered to sweep through an area that was a mile or so south of the airbase. We were supposed to cut bamboo poles and poke the earth as we moved forward on line. It was a totally crazy idea. But we had to follow orders. So, once we arrived at our LZ we cut as many poles as we could, we got on line, and then we began to move slowly forward…poking the sandy earth as we progressed. I felt ridiculous.

The morning sun rose in a clear blue sky. The temperature also rose. It was soon over a hundred degrees. We were sweating heavily. Our utilities were soaked. Our brains were cooking inside our helmets. Poke, poke, poke…. It was another miserable day in Vietnam.

A guy named Peter Ryan was to the left of me. He was slightly overweight, and he was paying a price for being out of shape. I could tell he was having difficulty. The unrelenting heat was wearing him out. As I walked along, poking the sandy earth, he suddenly collapsed. He lost consciousness and fell face first. I ran over to see if I could help him. But there was really nothing I could do. He passed out due to heat prostration. He needed to be moved into the shade. He needed to be doused with cool water. His high body temperature needed to be brought down before it caused some damage. I called for our platoon corpsman. A few seconds later he arrived.

"We'd better get him evacuated as soon as possible," our corpsman said. "His high temperature is dangerous. He might even die if we don't get him to the hospital in a hurry."

After our platoon commander arrived on the scene he called for a medevac. Everybody stopped moving forward and poking the ground with their poles. Maybe ten minutes later a chopper arrived. We loaded Peter aboard. He was still unconscious. A few minutes later the chopper flew away. And that was the last I ever saw of him. He never came back. I don't know what happened to him. I don't know if he lived…or died.

Early that afternoon someone in my squad poked the earth and something didn't sound right. Instead of the mushy sound that sand makes, there was a hard clatter that was typical of wood. A few more pokes, and a sheet of plywood was discovered just beneath a few inches of sand. After the sheet of plywood was lifted up, the entrance to an underground bunker was revealed. Maybe poking the earth with bamboo poles wasn't as stupid as I thought.

Our line came to a halt. Our platoon commander suddenly appeared. He got down on his knees and gazed into the tunnel for a minute or so. Then he stood up and had a brief conversation with our Vietnamese interpreter. A moment or two later, the interpreter kneeled down and shouted into the tunnel in Vietnamese. I assume he was telling anyone in the bunker to give up, and come out, or they would be killed. Nothing happened. No one emerged. The interpreter then relayed his message a second time, and he received the same non-response.

As this initial reaction to our discovery was gaining momentum, several women appeared in front of a nearby house. One was old, and one was young. The old woman had black teeth from chewing on betel nut. They both looked nervous. They were paying close attention. Their behavior suggested that the bunker was occupied. But we didn't know for certain. It was a guessing game.

Our platoon commander called for Jimmy Mitchell to come up. He was the smallest guy in our platoon. And because of his size, he had become our tunnel rat. The Lieutenant and Jimmy had a brief conversation. Then the Lieutenant pulled his forty-five out of his holster and gave it to Jimmy. He also handed him a flashlight. Jimmy lay down his rifle. Then he took off his pack, and his cartridge belt.

Jimmy had been ordered to crawl down the tunnel to check things out. Before he disappeared, he retrieved a hand grenade from a pouch on his cartridge belt. Then, a few seconds later, he disappeared. He just crawled into the tunnel like everything was perfectly normal. He showed no sign of fear. Maybe he expected the bunker to be empty. They usually were. But this time around things were different.

About ten seconds after he disappeared I heard a muted series of pistol shots. Then I saw Jimmy trying to get out of the tunnel. He was in a real panic. He was standing up, and almost clear when a hand grenade went off somewhere behind him…back down in the bunker. There was a sudden explosion of dust and Jimmy was hit by shrapnel. It peppered his legs. His back was protected by his flak jacket. He fell forward. He was quickly pulled out of the tunnel by our Lieutenant, and a couple of guys who were standing nearby. They lay him down on his stomach. He was in a lot of pain. He squirmed and kicked until our corpsman gave him a shot of morphine to kill the pain and calm him down. Our platoon commander called for another medevac.

While we patiently waited for the chopper, our Lieutenant decided to toss a CS gas grenade down the tunnel. He thought that if anyone was still alive, the teargas would force them to surrender. But nothing happened. Nobody came out of the bunker. Jimmy seemed to have killed whoever was down there with his pistol and the grenade that he threw. Throwing the grenade was a very dangerous thing to do. Jimmy was lucky to still be alive.

The two women in front of the house began to weep and wail. They knew that whoever was down in the bunker was dead. They wrung their hands, wiped tears from their eyes, and cried out in Vietnamese. We ignored them. Pity was in short supply.

After the chopper picked Jimmy up, our Lieutenant decided to bring the whole lousy affair to a dramatic end. We had several engineers with us. They had twenty pound satchel charges composed of C4 that were specifically designed to destroy various kinds of bunkers. After our Lieutenant told everyone to get back a safe distance, an engineer lit the fuse on a satchel charge, and then yelled fire in the hole three times. Then he threw the charge into the tunnel. A minute or so later there was a tremendous explosion. A big cloud of sand erupted skywards. The explosion left a crater that was about ten feet deep and twenty feet across. In the bottom of the crater lay a number of bodies that had been torn to shreds. Bloody arms and legs were mixed with the twisted remains of their weapons. I had no idea why the VC didn't surrender when they had the chance. They chose to die when they could have gone on living. I was afraid that my squad would be ordered to retrieve what was left of the VC, to verify the body count. Luckily that didn't happen. Another squad was ordered to do the bloody task. It took about twenty minutes. Arms and legs were placed in one pile, heads and torsos in another, and weapons in a third. Counting the bodies seemed pointless. But I guess our battalion commander needed to know with certainty how many VC had been killed. Four was the answer. Then our line began to move forward once again. The show was over. We left the piles of mangled flesh sitting on the edge of the crater. We never found the mortars.

A Thousand Cuts

There was always another patrol to go on. This was all we could do to try and control the movement of VC through the local villages. And, in many ways, our patrols were a waste of time. The villagers knew we were coming and they'd sound the alarm. They'd beat on a tin can to warn their neighbors. As a consequence, we never surprised the VC. They always surprised us. One or two snipers would often take a few potshots at the guys in our patrols. Or, a slightly larger group of VC would spring an ambush. They always got the first shot. And we were always at a disadvantage because we didn't know the neighborhood. Nevertheless, the game went on.

The war I fought in Vietnam was death by a thousand cuts. It was based on tactics at the squad and fire team level. By the middle of 1967 that changed. The Marines moved north to the DMZ. From that time on they fought a war that was more conventional than guerrilla. They fought with North Vietnamese Army regulars. They battled to control the high ground. And battalion size units were often involved. This later version of the war didn't revolve around villages and rice paddies. The earlier war that I fought, was a wait and see kind of experience. You knew you were going to be shot at, but you never knew when or where. My war was full of sudden shocks. And if the snipers didn't wound or kill you, there were always lots of mines and booby traps to deal with.

The first time I was shot at was almost comical. My squad leader, Corporal James, discovered a small crop of sugarcane in a village. He took out his K-bar and hacked down a few pieces to hand to the guys in our patrol. When we peeled off the rough bark, there was a nice white interior that was very sweet. After everyone had a piece of sugar cane, our patrol went on its way. We munched on the sugar cane as we walked along. Nobody thought there would be trouble. We hadn't been in Vietnam very long, and the VC were still an unknown force to be reckoned with. Up to that point, I had been on a number of patrols, and there had been no contact at all. They were like long boring walks in the park.

Three days before the patrol, we had swept through a large village that was partially surrounded by sandy flat lands. Our sweep ended on a large sand dune that featured an old French bunker. It was made out of concrete. It was positioned to oversee the village and the open area we had just passed through. We set up in a defensive perimeter around the bunker. And then we dug foxholes. Coming through the village two guys in our sister platoon had stepped on booby traps. They were badly injured…so I heard through the grapevine.

The second night in our new perimeter we received some sniper fire from the village. In response, our platoon commander, Lieutenant Dawson, ordered an 81mm mortar crew to lob a few rounds at the sniper. This put an end to the harassment. The rest of the night was quiet. Early the next morning my fire team was ordered to go into the village to see if the sniper had been killed. The chances of that happening were low. But it was still worth a look. My squad leader, Corporal James, came along out of curiosity.

And so, munching on sticks of sugarcane, the guys in my patrol moved right along. As things turned out, concentrating on eating the sugarcane was not a good idea. This was our first mistake. Corporal James had been foolish. To compound the situation, I made the second mistake. I was walking point. I took a path across a clear, sandy area. When the entire patrol was fully exposed, a sniper, probably the same one that had shot at us the night before, suddenly opened fire.

I dropped my piece of sugarcane. Then I ran toward the safety of a house that was not too far away. I wanted to get out of the clear area. I could hear the bullets snapping by. They were very close. I know the sniper was shooting at me because of the sound of the bullets. When they snap by like small firecrackers, this means that you are the target. After I reached the house, I looked back and was horrified to see that everyone in the patrol had hit the deck in the middle of the sandy area. They had no cover at all. And they were shooting in every possible direction. It was crazy as hell! They didn't know what they were shooting at. They had no target. Nobody knew where the sniper was. And, after fifteen or so long seconds, the sniper stopped shooting and slipped away. He didn't hit anyone. But he definitely woke us up. We were very lucky. Our stupidity could have been tragic. From then on, whenever I walked point, I tried to take a route that provided good cover. And if there was a clear area we had to cross, I'd bring everyone up on line so their weapons were pointed forward to provide covering fire…if it was necessary. Then I'd send one or two men across the clear area at a time. I never screwed around again. I never let down my guard.

We were on edge for the rest of the patrol. Everyone paid attention. As we circled back through the village toward our perimeter on the sand dune, we encountered an old woman who was holding the severed leg of a pig. Our mortar fire from the night before hadn't killed the sniper. It killed her pig. It blew off one of its front legs. She was very angry at us. She was waving the bloody leg, and yelling in Vietnamese. I didn't know what to do or say. So I didn't do or say anything. We just went on our way. Steve was behind me. I could hear him laughing at the old woman. We were short on sympathy. No doubt the people in her village were collaborating with the VC. The sniper was probably related to her family. And we also knew that the villagers had helped the VC install booby traps. If they had killed a Marine, we would have burned her village to the ground as punishment. The war was hard on everyone and everything…even pigs.

Infanticide

Our column was composed of three Amtrack with a tank in the lead. The three squads that composed my platoon were divided among the Amtrack. We were riding on top, instead of inside, because it was so hot. The rice paddies we moved through were dry and dusty. It was mid-summer. Suddenly, as we approached a small village, we began to receive small arms fire. We jumped off the amtrack and ran to form a skirmish line behind a large rice paddy dike. Then the guys in my platoon got down and returned fire. My fire team ended up on the far right flank of the line in a position that was exposed…although I didn't know it. I was sitting with my back against a high dike. I thought I was safe. I was smoking a cigarette while the firefight went on. The guys in my fire team were not in a position to shoot back. Suddenly, there was an explosion of dirt and I felt a sharp blow to the ribs on my right side. It took a few moments for me to realize that I'd just been shot. I reached inside my flak jacket feeling for a wound. Luckily, a panel in my flak jacket stopped the bullet, which had ricocheted off the ground. I could hear bullets snapping by. I immediately lay down on my belly. I made as small a target as I could. A moment later there was another explosion of dirt. I felt a sharp blow. A small hole appeared in the right shoulder of my flak jacket. I realized I'd been shot again. This time the bullet, which was also a ricochet, had creased my shoulder. The VC soldier was shooting low. Otherwise, I would have been badly wounded. I immediately jumped up and dove over the same rice paddy dike I'd just been leaning against. I was trying to avoid being hit again. I could hear Jason screaming for the Corpsman. He thought I'd been shot in the head. A short time later Doc Watson arrived. He got really angry when he looked at my shoulder because the wound was so minor.

"I can't believe I ran across that fucking rice paddy under fire to take care of a wound this trivial," he yelled. Then he covered the wound with a large band aid.

"I didn't yell for you to come," I said. "It wasn't my fault."

But I don't think he heard me. He was rattled by all the small arms fire. Having treated my insignificant wound he quickly made his way back to the front of our line.

Then the tank opened fire. For some reason that I've never understood, they fired a single round at a small blue house that was made out of concrete block. It was a nice house…relatively speaking. Usually, village houses were primitive structures made out of bamboo. This house stood apart. The round from the tank knocked a hole in one wall of the house that was about three feet in diameter.

By this time our firefight had dwindled into sporadic fire. It was a clear signal that the VC, having rattled our nerves, were beginning to pull out.

Then I saw a woman with a baby emerge from the blue house. She was walking directly into the space between us and the VC. She was stumbling and weaving back and forth. She was clearly shell shocked from the tank fire. An instant later my platoon commander called for my fire team to come up.

"Get that woman out of there," he yelled.

So, following orders, me, Steve, and Jason ran out in front of our line to help the woman and her baby get to safety. They helped the woman. I took her baby away from her to make things go faster and easier. When I looked down at the child I could see that it was bleeding from its ears and nose. It was also very, very quiet. Its eyes were closed. Both the woman and her child were suffering from concussion. That pointless round from the tank had done a lot of unnecessary damage. There was no small arms fire coming from that blue house. I was afraid that the baby was dead.

Once we passed back through our line I gave the baby to Doc Watson. I was hoping he could do something to save the baby. Then my fire team returned to its position on the line. The firefight was over. The only real casualties were the woman and her baby. Both of them were evacuated by helicopter a short time later. When I talked with Doc Watson later that day, he told me the baby was dead.

That was the day I really began to hate the war. I hated what it was doing to us and the people of Vietnam. It was nothing but a cold, impersonal machine that ran on haphazard violence. The war was an ongoing series of horrific surprises. There was absolutely nothing you could be certain about…except for uncertainty itself. I began to hate myself. I was trapped. By turning the Vietnamese into our enemy, we turned ourselves into animals. And there was a vicious, cruel irony to the war. We were killing the same people we were supposed to be saving from the tyranny of communism. After the incident with the baby, I began to feel like a Nazi. The war was nothing but a shit show. I don't think the war, with its promise of democracy, was worth the life of that small baby. We destroyed millions of people, and in the process, we saved no one…not even ourselves.

Oneness

I spent a large part of my time in the country sitting on the edge of a foxhole staring at the land, the sky, and the stars, as one day after another passed slowly by. If my outfit wasn't on the move, if I wasn't walking another patrol, if I wasn't sitting quietly in an ambush site, if I wasn't riding a chopper to another LZ, I sat in silence and surveyed my surroundings. I was constantly on guard. I hoped to see the VC before they opened fire. But that never happened. Not even once. They always got the first shot. In fact, during my entire tour of duty, I never once saw a live VC. All I saw were VC that were dead.

My life was very simple. I was in touch with the earth twenty-four hours a day. I slept on the earth. I slept in the rain. My feet were usually wet from the rice paddies, or the puddle of muddy water in the bottom of a foxhole. My utilities were streaked with mud. I wore the earth like a Halloween mask composed of dirt. We didn't have access to showers, so our bodies stank from sweat. We were not walking upon the earth and separate from it. We were joined to the earth. We became an indivisible part of the earth. We dug our foxholes in the earth, and we depended on the earth to protect us, to conceal us. We were like wild animals. We were like predators. We used the earth to hunt and kill. The earth was our trusted ally. And as the war progressed, and the spirit of Mister Death drifted like a cold breeze across the killing fields, the earth was life itself.

And the villagers were also close to the earth. The Vietnamese who tended the rice paddies belonged to the landscape the way clouds belong to the sky. They also lived simple lives. The homes they lived in were constructed of basic plant material, bamboo and thatch, with dirt floors and walls that were open to the breeze. Most villages had a common well, and a ditch that was used as a public toilet. Everything in a Vietnamese village was close to the earth. The water buffalo, the chickens and ducks, the dogs and the children, they all seemed perfectly natural. They belonged to the earth.

And the earth was green. It was so green that it seemed to emit a form of radiant energy. It was unreal. And the green infused everything, the rice paddies, the villages, the gardens, the trees and bushes, and the hills and mountains that rose up west of Danang. That's where the jungle began. Giant trees formed on the hills like fur on an animal's back. And that's where the green reached its highest and most pure state. When we passed into the jungle we became intimate with the color. It surrounded us. We moved into a thick maze of plants that formed a wall so dense that we had to stay on a trail to make progress. The plant life channeled us like water in a ditch. It imposed limits on our ability to move freely, to make choices. If we got off the trail it would be slow going. On the other hand, if we followed the trail, we knew we would eventually walk into a VC ambush. They would hide in the bushes just off the trail. Then, in a split second, all hell would break loose. The VC would rattle our cage. Their small arms fire would erupt in the midst of the green maze. Men would be wounded or killed. And then, after the VC melted back into the jungle, an anxious silence would fill the air with dread.

In passing through the jungle I used to imagine that I was an animal. I felt like I was crawling through the green sea of plants stalking my prey. My motion felt natural. I felt like I belonged in the jungle. I carried my rifle with my right hand. It became an extension of my body. As I passed through the jungle the facade of civilized behavior was wiped away like dust from a tabletop. There is nothing civilized about war. War is the antithesis of civility. In truth, I had become a savage, living according to a different set of rules that were all based on survival. Rule one: pay attention. Rule two: pay attention. Rule three: pay attention…. I wanted to kill the enemy to placate my fear of a violent death.

In the jungle, I felt like I was passing through a world that was millions of years old. We were just the latest tourists to make a visit. The jungle felt timeless compared to my own transitory existence. It also had a passive, indifferent nature. It was neither for, nor against our presence. In the long term, what difference did it make if some young Marine shed his red blood in the midst of all that greenery? The jungle was indifferent to death. In fact, death was part of its life cycle. Death was necessary. So what difference did it make if bombs and artillery shells blew craters in the earth and tore the limbs off the trees? In the long run the jungle would heal itself. Its great strength was phenomenal growth and abundant life. Dropping a bomb on the jungle was like spitting into the ocean.

At night the jungle became a landscape filled with eerie shapes and objects. Mushrooms and fungus faintly glowed with phosphorescent light. There was a stillness in the air that was laced with nervous expectation, as if some monstrous creature was about to leap out of the shadows. What can one expect from the darkness but uncertainty and fear? And the jungle was always very dark at night. The triple canopy trees were like umbrellas that blocked the light of the moon and stars. When we were through humping for the day we settled into our defense perimeter. And because no fires were allowed, we ate a supper of cold C-rations. Then we set the watch. It was always fifty percent: one man on, one man asleep. We rose at first light, ate another cold meal, and then we saddled up and got underway. We went looking for Charlie. We were always looking for Charlie. And we knew that Charlie was looking for us. That was the lethal game of hide and seek we played.

One afternoon my entire company was in column on some muddy, slippery trail. We were going up a steep hill. Our progress was slow and awkward. I avoided the center of the trail to keep from slipping backward due to the mud. I chose to walk just off the trail where the footing among some low lying weeds was far better. Off to either side of the trail the jungle was so dense that we couldn't see farther than fifteen or twenty feet. Our vision was blocked by a jumbled wall of big leafy bushes and vines. We were spaced out in the column. Each man followed the man ahead with a safe space between them. If someone slipped and fell, which happened from time to time, I could hear them curse…in spite of our orders to remain silent.

"Motherfucking shit," they'd say angrily. "Where the fuck are we going?"

Nobody knew where we were at, or where we were going. And what difference would it have made if we knew the answer to those questions? We were in the jungle looking for Charlie. That was all that mattered. We followed behind one another and put our faith in our Company Commander, Captain Lawrence. He was the brains of the outfit. He had a map, a compass, and a radio. He was in touch with our battalion commander, who was in touch with our regimental commander, or was in touch with our division commander…and so it went from low to high. We assumed that someone knew what they were doing. And that their superior knowledge would keep us from being bushwhacked by the VC. In truth, we were expected to make contact. That was the whole point of our operation. We were supposed to go into the jungle and walk around to make targets out of ourselves. Then, when Charlie decided to open fire, we would know his location for at least five minutes. And this might give us enough time to call in artillery or an airstrike.

After being seriously defeated in several large scale battles, our enemy decided to break up into small units. Then they resorted to hit and run tactics. Small units are much easier to handle. They can come and go without exposing themselves. Relying on ambushes, they could inflict casualties, and then rapidly disappear. This was the nature of the war we fought in 1965 and 1966. It was all about quick hits, and equally quick getaways. And the VC were experts at this game. We were fighting against shadows. It was a war that was hard on your nerves.

Every time we went out on a patrol or a search and destroy operation, we expected to be surprised. We knew the VC were going to get the first shot. They not only knew the neighborhood, they were an integral part of it. They could hide amongst the population. This was, perhaps, the greatest problem we faced. How do you separate a rice farmer from a VC soldier? It was a situation that produced a monumental level of paranoia. As time passed, and the war went on, we realized that we couldn't trust anyone among the villagers. If they didn't participate directly in the fire fights we were in, they planted booby traps. And, whenever we entered a village, no one offered to tell us where those booby traps were located. Their silence was a form of support for the VC. In the end, we painted the villagers with a very broad brush. We considered them all to be VC supporters. That simplified the problem. And it became the rationale behind our widespread use of Zippo cigarette lighters. Out in the countryside, there were no friendly villagers. The VC controlled everyone, and everything. We were in control of nothing at all.

In any event, as our company's lead fire team approached the top of the muddy hill, they were suddenly ambushed. A sergeant who was walking point, was shot through the chest. The man behind him was shot through the stomach. The platoon leader was shot through the head and died instantly. An ARVN trooper who was behind the lieutenant was shot through the leg. The whole nasty ambush lasted about fifteen seconds. Then, before we could go on the offense, the VC disappeared back into the jungle and left us twisting in the wind.

My platoon was bringing up the rear of the column, so we were never directly involved in the brief firefight. All we did was move off the trail a few feet and hit the deck. There were no enemy targets for us to shoot at. So we just lay still and waited. Maybe ten or fifteen minutes after the shooting stopped, we got up, and then we began to move forward once again. When the company reached the top of the hill, we set up a defense perimeter. Then we called for a medevac chopper. After it arrived, it couldn't land because of the trees, so it went into a prolonged hover. Then it sent down a cable attached to a wire basket in the shape of a human body. It took about twenty minutes to evacuate our dead and wounded. Then we were ordered to dig in. We were, for the time being at least, staying put.

We expected sniper fire. But that never happened. I guess Charlie decided to quit while he was ahead. After two quiet days we were ordered to head back down the hill toward the distant rice paddies in the flatland. We were going to be lifted back to our platoon position south of Danang. The operation was over. The abysmal score for our effort favored the VC.

To win a war I think you have to force your enemy to submit. You have to think one step ahead, and control everything that takes place. War, first of all, is a game of control. You have to control the land, and the people who live on the land. Then too, maybe winning is a question of determination. Looking back, I don't think we followed any of these rules. In fact, I don't think we could follow these rules because we were always on the defense. We were never in control of anything for long. And no matter how many battles we won, we were always destined to lose the war. The VC knew exactly what they were fighting for. And they were far more determined to win. In our heart of hearts, I don't think we gave a shit about who was going to win. We just wanted to survive. And that's not enough to win a war. Fighting in order to survive is not the same thing as fighting to save your country. I think we always knew that our effort was pointless, that our goal of protecting the democratic south was tainted by corruption, lies, and paranoid delusions. We were not defending the United States. The VC were never a threat to our country. The Vietnamese were fighting a civil war. And, in the main, they wanted a country that was free of colonialism, and that was unified. They wanted their own independent oneness. That was their simple goal. And to achieve it, they were willing to fight to the death. Our goal was nothing but a bad joke. On our side, nobody wanted to die in the defense of South Vietnam. And wanting to die for the greater glory of the Corps was incredibly stupid. So, we just counted the days until our tour of duty was over, and we could go home, and try to forget the war.

Ambush

Manny Alberto was a squared away Marine. He was a hard charger. He did everything well. He followed orders without complaining. He understood small unit tactics. He was responsible. And he wanted to succeed. He wanted to win the war. Several months after we entered the country, our platoon commander promoted him to corporal, and made him a squad leader. Manny was also a good friend. We had gone out on liberty a number of times when we were stationed at Camp Pendleton. And, while our platoon was standing guard on the airbase, Manny and I had a chance to go into Danang. We decided to avoid the whore houses and bars in favor of a Vietnamese restaurant. It was located in a large house that was slightly run down. It looked more European than Vietnamese. After we found a table to sit at, a good looking young woman came over to take our order. She spoke excellent English, which made her all the more attractive. Manny's eyes lit up.

"You speak very good English," he said, after he placed his order. "You must have studied in school."

"I was a student of foreign languages," she said. "I also speak French."

Then she disappeared to give our orders to the cook.

"She's interesting," Manny said. "I'd like to talk with her. She's the first Vietnamese woman I've met who speaks good English."

Maybe ten minutes later she returned with our food. The restaurant was fairly empty. There were few customers, so Manny asked her to join us. At first she seemed a little bit reluctant, but eventually she gave in, and sat down at our table. After Manny and I introduced ourselves we shook her hand. Her name was Lien.

"How long have you been in my country?" She wanted to know.

"About three months," Manny said.

"That's not long," she said. "Since you Americans arrived everything is changing. Day by day the war is getting worse."

"We can handle it," Manny said, like a good Marine. "With luck it will soon be over. We are going to beat the VC, and free South Vietnam from the communists. It shouldn't take too long"

"I don't think beating the VC will be that easy," she said quietly. "I think the war is going to go on for a long, long time. Your enemy is determined. They will not give up easily."

I was somewhat surprised by her prediction. She seemed to know something that we were missing entirely. Indirectly, she was saying that we were naïve. And, I suppose, it was true. We were brainwashed with American idealism and esprit de corps. While she was just slightly older than us, she seemed to be a whole lot wiser. And, I think her wisdom, her understanding of reality, made her sad. I could see it in her eyes. The war was a burden that she, and the Vietnamese, had to carry with them from one day to the next. It was inescapable.

"Are you married?" Manny asked, changing the subject. His curiosity was leading the way.

"No," she said. "My husband is dead. He was a helicopter pilot. The VC shot him down."

There was a pause in the conversation that suddenly took on weight and density. Things were becoming very personal, very quick.

"I'm so sorry," Manny said. "I'm sorry I asked the question. It's none of my business."

Manny didn't anticipate her answer. It came as a mild shock. It took the conversation in a direction he didn't want to go. Instead of sunshine and happiness, he found himself in darkness and grief.

"Don't be sorry," she said. "My country is at war and people die all the time. Grief has become part of our lives. We are helpless. We are at the mercy of the Americans, and the North Vietnamese. Our future is filled with death and destruction. There's nothing we can do to stop the insanity. In the end, I think everyone will lose."

"I hope we can change things for the better," Manny said. "That's why we're here. That's what we're fighting for."

"If you succeed, what will be the cost?" She asked. "How many innocent people will die?"

Neither Manny, nor I, had an answer to that question. Our entry into the conflict had just begun. We envisioned a war that was clean, that spared the innocent, and only destroyed the enemy. We were the good guys. We wore white hats and we always won the fight. In reality, we were innocent young men, blinded by our youthful optimism, and entirely ignorant of the reality we were facing. War and innocence don't get along at all.

After she wished us well, our conversation came to an end. Then she stood up and went back to work.

"She's a nice woman," Manny said. "I feel sorry for her. I feel sorry for this country. What can we do but fight the war? We don't have a choice. And she doesn't have a choice either. Everything is fucked up."

I couldn't disagree.

Several days later Manny took his squad out on an ambush patrol. He left our line just after dark. Then Manny walked the patrol to a location that was next to a dirt path. Remaining silent was very important. No loud talking was allowed. His men communicated by whispers. After they arrived at the ambush site, they set up on line, parallel to the path, in a spot with good cover. Obviously, they wanted to remain unseen. Then they lay down on their bellies with their ten rifles pointed at the path for the rest of the night. No one was allowed to sleep. The watch was always set at one hundred percent. Lying in an ambush requires a lot of patience. Out of boredom, a few guys might roll onto their back, and then observe the stars and the moon overhead. They might think about their home, their girlfriend, and what they were going to do with their lives after the war. The silence, and the darkness, forced everyone to turn inward. Self-reflection was a predictable response. It was a way to pass the time.

The vast majority of ambushes we set up were duds. Nothing ever happened. The enemy never showed up. The moon rose in the night sky. And the moon went down. And then, before first light, the squad would get up and make its way back to the platoon perimeter. Then someone in the patrol would fire off a green flare to let the guys on the line know that they were friendly. And, minutes later, they'd be back from a long night that was spent doing nothing at all…unless they made contact.

About two o'clock in the morning the guys in Manny's squad heard a noise on the path. It was the distinct sound of footsteps approaching. They couldn't tell whether it was one person, or a group. They waited. Everyone took their rifles off safety. They prepared to open fire. Manny thought it was the VC. Who else would be out walking around in the early morning? There was a curfew in effect. All the villagers in the area knew about it. They knew the Marines were active at night. They knew that it was very dangerous to be out of their houses. Only the VC moved around at night. Snipers would take advantage of the dark to find a good position. Then, after sunrise, they'd fire two or three shots at our line before they disappeared. They never hit anyone. And we never returned fire. We didn't want to give our positions away. So we ignored the snipers. They were more of a nuisance than a serious threat.

Manny waited. The footsteps grew closer. He could tell that it was a group. But he didn't know how many men there were. Everyone in his squad was wide awake. They prepared to open fire the moment the group was inside of their kill zone. His squad was set in about five feet from the path so their fire would be very accurate. They would be shooting at point blank range. It would be hard to miss their targets.

As Manny and his squad patiently waited to spring the ambush, the first man in the approaching group entered the kill zone. The guy was more shadow than substance. The darkness made seeing details impossible. Then a second guy appeared, followed by a third, and a forth, and a fifth…. They were clumped together and walking noisily, as if they didn't have a care in the world. In total, there were nine shadowy figures. They were all bunched together.

Manny's squad opened fire. It was a tremendous volley. It went on until everyone in the passing group was lying dead or wounded on the path. Then Manny's guys shot at the fallen bodies. It was a massacre. The men in the shadowy group never knew what hit them. They never even shot back. They just fell down dead and wounded. Nobody escaped.

After the last shot had been fired, Manny emerged from his position. Then he carefully approached the group of men lying on the path. As he drew near, he discovered that the fallen men were wearing uniforms and helmets. They also had packs and cartridge belts. They carried American made weapons. Alarm bells began to go off. As things turned out, Manny's squad had ambushed a group of ARVN troops. They were our friendly allies. Manny was stunned. What were ARVN troops doing out walking around in the early morning hours? Where were they going? Where were they coming from? Their presence on the path was inexplicable. Things like this were not supposed to happen. The Marines, and the ARVN, were supposed to coordinate their activities. It was a nightmare. Manny, the hard charging Marine, had taken out nine men who were on our side of the war.

Manny had a radio. He called in and reported the contact. He told our company commander what had happened. In response, our company commander went out to the ambush site to check everything out. After he arrived, he called for two medevac choppers to take away the dead and wounded. He listened patiently while Manny explained exactly what happened.

Later that day, when Manny came back to our perimeter, he was a nervous wreck. Eventually, he would be transferred out of our unit and placed in a rear echelon job. He would never be charged with a crime. The whole sad affair would be dismissed as a friendly fire accident. It was just one of those tragic events that can happen when young men go into combat.

Monsoon

To keep our cigarettes dry we put them inside our helmets. That was the only place that was dry. Every other place on our bodies was going to get soaked through and through…in spite of the ponchos we wore. They were supposed to be waterproof, but that was a joke. Going out on patrol in the monsoon rain was like stepping into a shower on full blast. It was unrelenting, almost Biblical. It made me think about Noah's ark. The rain flooded the rice paddies. It turned them into waist deep ponds that we had to wade across when we went out on patrol. The sound of the rain when it hit the flooded rice paddies was like bacon sizzling in a frying pan.

Our commanders pulled us back to guard the perimeter of the airbase at the beginning of the monsoon. They were afraid of another sapper attack. My platoon was assigned an area that was on the northern end of the airstrip. Because of the daily rain, we actually got large tents to live in. It was a big improvement over the sandbag bunkers we had been living in.

When we were stationed a few miles south of the airbase we received fairly regular sniper fire. Maybe two or three shots a day. We never caught the sniper. He was a bad shot. So we mostly ignored him. Some of the guys would remain standing and talking as the sniper's bullets whizzed by. Once the monsoon began, all the sniper fire came to a sudden end. I guess Charlie didn't like getting soaked any more than we did.

Going out on fire team patrols north of the airbase was miserable. We had to stay off the bumpy dirt road that ran straight out from the north gate. We didn't want to make clear targets of ourselves. So when we went on patrol we took the scenic route. We jumped over fences, passed through gardens, forced our way through hedges, and we used tree lines for concealment. We were never shot at. The rain was our only enemy. It also brought out hungry leeches. After we completed our patrol, and we were back inside our tent, we had to burn the leeches off our feet and legs. The leeches were swollen with blood. They looked like small black cigars. When we stepped on them, they'd squirt out a thin stream of blood. You couldn't feel them sucking your blood because they emitted an anesthetic when they bit into your flesh. But once they were fat and swollen, then you could feel them squishing around in your boots. The leeches loved the rain. Their numbers increased dramatically. And after we used a cigarette to burn them off, they left a small, slightly bloody hole in your skin. And, over time, this tiny wound might get infected. If it did, then jungle rot would set in. This was a biological infection that created large circular sores that were caked with puss. A number of the guys came down with these ugly sores, including myself. During the monsoon we also stopped going out on search and destroy operations. Visibility was so bad our choppers couldn't fly. And, without our choppers, we were immobile. We sat around in our tent, read books, played card games, and we cleaned and oiled our rifles and magazines. We had to be constantly on guard for the buildup of rust. Everything was damp, and smelled of mold, and mildew.

One pleasant discovery that we made, while we were patrolling the neighborhood, was a small, inconspicuous, house of prostitution. It was just off the dirt road that ran to and from the airbase. It was partially hidden by a few trees and bushes. After we made the discovery, a lot of guys became very enthusiastic about going out on patrol. The house was always open for business. I can remember dropping in around two o'clock in the morning…just to escape from the rain for a few minutes. The women were young and lively. And, while we couldn't speak Vietnamese, and they couldn't speak much English, we didn't have a problem communicating with each other. Our lives were being lived at some sort of instinctual level. They were three dollar whores. Yes, and no, was the only English required. The girls managed to stay busy. It wasn't uncommon to drop in and find another fire team patrol in the house. Things could get crowded. While we were in the house we posted a sentry to be on the lookout for our company commander. During the day, he sometimes drove his mighty mite down the dirt road to check everything out. We didn't want to get caught hiding in a whorehouse, when we were supposed to be protecting the airbase from Charlie. As far as I know, nobody ever got caught. Our sentry always did an excellent job. If he spotted our company commander he'd run into the house and give the alarm. In a matter of two seconds everyone would vacate the house and we'd disappear into the bushy landscape. I'm not even certain that our company commander knew the whorehouse existed. He never stopped there. If he knew, he never said anything.

Prostitution and war go hand in hand. In Greek myth, Aphrodite, the goddess of sensual love, is the lover of Mars, the god of war. All the fighting and dying seems to intensify the need to make contact with the opposite sex. Maybe it has something to do with an overabundance of testosterone? In any event, women are not the least bit stupid. They know a good market when they see it. On the demand side of the equation, there are hundreds of thousands of horny soldiers caught up in the life and death struggle of the meat grinder. On the supply side there are thousands of prostitutes. And selling themselves to soldiers, in many instances, may be an act of desperation that enables a woman to buy food for her family. But I also suspect that the pleasure principle is involved. During World War Two, I'm sure there was a lot of prostitution going on in England, France, Italy, Holland, and even Germany after Hitler bit the dust. War reduces everyone it touches to the basic level of mere survival. And, if you have nothing left but a sexy body, you are going to do whatever is necessary to stay alive. War also turns everyone it touches into an animal. And I think that some men and women actually enjoy living life at this level. Getting laid is a simple transaction. There are no emotional bonds. It's just a business deal that takes care of a very basic, very natural need. I think the only time I ever felt like a human being was when I was with a prostitute, laughing and joking, and having sex. Otherwise, as Marines we were locked into our role as tough guys. And, to be honest, we were always afraid of being afraid. We could never take off the mask. Being with a woman, even a prostitute, was antidotal to our pretense of fearlessness. We could relax for a while. And no doubt hundreds of thousands of guys found a warm sanctuary while lying between the open thighs of a prostitute. For just three dollars you could escape from the war and pretend that your life made sense. Life without pleasure has no meaning at all.

Hatred

As the war went on and on, I began to form a very negative view of the human condition. As an aggressive species, I could easily see that we are destined to fight one war, after another. Our history on this planet is an intermittent record of war. And my sense of hopelessness was enhanced by the ever gray sterility of my environment, its one dimensional reality of violence and death. In a combat zone there was nothing to appreciate, to enjoy, or to like and love. There was only the nihilistic emptiness of going on with your life out of fear. I felt like I was living in a nightmare, in a world that was devoid of anything I could look forward to with pleasure. I was starved for meaning. As a result, I began to hate everything. It was a natural response. It was probably a kind of self-defense that allowed me to put some distance between myself, and the impersonal brutality of the war. A human life wasn't worth much in Vietnam. And even as I participated in killing other human beings, I wouldn't let myself believe that I was actually involved. The experience seemed to belong to a stranger. I was deceiving myself to remain sane. I lied to myself in order to protect myself. There was some small part of my mind that wanted to remain innocent…even in the midst of madness and mayhem. And so, I hated everything connected to the war. But I kept my hatred to myself for the most part. Complaining wouldn't change anything for the better.

I hated Vietnam. I hated the rice paddies. I hated the villages. I hated the heat. I hated fire fights. I hated the jungle. I hated going out on patrol. I hated going on search and destroy operations. I hated taking orders. I hated giving orders. I hated my rifle and my hand grenades. I hated my muddy boots. I hated my helmet. I hated my pack. I hated going without a shower. I hated eating C-rations. I hated standing watch. I hated the bugs. I hated booby traps. I hated snipers. I hated to be ambushed. I hated the politicians that had ordered us to fight and die. And I hated losing my friends. In essence, I hated the war. I think my hatred was an indirect way of hanging onto my memory of civilization and everything it has to offer. I mean peace and security. I mean love and kindness. I mean freedom from repression. I mean the freedom to speak your mind. For the guys that fought the war none of these things existed in Vietnam. We were puppets of the green machine. Your personal feelings didn't count at all. They were irrelevant. I once talked to Corporal James about how I really felt. He spent several years in college before he volunteered to join the Marines. I think his brief fling with higher education gave him a rational basis for understanding and insight. Corporal James was a rare young man. He was a good squad leader.

"It doesn't matter how you feel," he said. "We have a job to do that's more important than your feelings. Your feelings arise from your individuality, your sense of self, and your need for pleasure and satisfaction. They are also a personal reaction to fear and adversity. But they have no bearing whatsoever on your role as a Marine in a platoon…which is far more important. Your personal feelings won't keep you alive. Only the support of the platoon can do that. And, in order to belong, you have to sacrifice your individuality and your feelings. You have to become one with the group. Whatever happens, you can't let the group down. Like it or not you have to play your part. It's a matter of life and death."

"It's hard to do," I said. "How can anyone do what we do on a daily basis without hating everything this war stands for?"

"If you didn't hate this war, you'd be insane," he said. "Hatred and fear are rational responses to combat. I wouldn't want to serve with anyone who didn't hate this fucking war. But your hatred doesn't matter. It's pointless."

My hatred was so strong and general that I even hated one of my fellow Marines. He was a big muscular guy named Alex Crawford. He was our platoon psychopath. He had no conscience. He was also a bully. He constantly tried to intimidate the other Marines in our unit. We had a Jewish guy in our platoon named Sheldon Abrams that Alex mercilessly picked on.

"All you Jews care about is money," Alex would say loudly. "You don't give a shit about anything else. So how did you end up in the Marine Corps you greedy motherfucker? How did you survive boot camp? You're as out of place as tits on a boar hog."

Sheldon was a guy who had a slight, medium build. Alex outweighed him by fifty pounds at least. So the idea that Sheldon could take on Alex in a fistfight was ridiculous. Sheldon had to knuckle under to the abuse, as did a number of other Marines in my outfit. Alex was a real problem. He was bad for morale. I hated him so much that I actually had fantasies about killing him. I wanted to toss a hand grenade into his foxhole in the middle of the night. If I could have done it, without getting caught, I may have followed through. The idea of bringing justice to Alex was very appealing.

One night Alex took his fire team out on a patrol. He led his men into a village that was about five hundred meters from our platoon perimeter. Then he searched the various houses looking for weapons. He woke the villagers up and ransacked their meager belongings. He terrified them. And somewhere along the way he took three young men into custody. They were the right age to be VC soldiers. And, as far as Alex was concerned, that was all that counted. At the point of his rifle he ordered them down to the edge of the nearby rice paddy. Then he forced them to kneel down. A moment later he opened fire and killed all three of them. I was on watch in my foxhole at the time. I saw a burst of red tracers ricocheting off the water in the rice paddy. The following morning I found out what happened. I was totally disgusted.

Alex liked violence. He liked killing. He liked exerting power over others. And he didn't care at all about minor details. In his simple brain, he thought that all the villagers were VC. As far as he was concerned that was the end of the story. Our platoon commander said nothing, and he did nothing. The murders were ignored.

Then, about three weeks later, Karma finally caught up with Alex. He had been berating and picking on the guys in his fire team and they were pissed off. Alex left his foxhole to set up a Claymore anti-personnel mine. He took the mine in his hands, and then he walked it out about fifty feet in front of the line. Then he set up a small tripod, attached the mine, and aimed it. Finally, he went to insert the blasting cap, which was attached to a wire that ran back to his foxhole. At the far end of the wire was a clapper. To set off the mine, you'd take the clapper in your hand, and then you'd squeeze it. This action sends an electrical charge down the wire to the blasting cap, which then explodes, setting off the mine. Apparently, so the story went, the guy in Alex's foxhole wasn't paying attention. The clapper fell into the bottom of the hole, and it was accidently stepped on. The blasting cap went off just as Alex was leaning over to insert it in the mine. It did not detonate the mine. But it did tear his face apart. And it damaged his eyes. The guy who stepped on the clapper didn't seem to be too upset about the accident. In fact, I thought he looked like a man who had just been pleasantly relieved of a serious problem.

Our platoon commander called in for another medevac. Ten minutes later we helped Alex climb aboard the chopper. He never came back. I have no idea what happened to him. That was a rare day in Vietnam. I actually had something to be happy about.

The Pile

It was the war alone that turned Vietnam into such an ugly country. It rapidly became a hideous combination of violence, death, and utter misery. Everyone and everything suffered. And the suffering cast a pall that diminished the natural beauty of the landscape. Minus the war, the country was a perfect subject for postcards. Strangely enough, Vietnam reminded me of Gauguin's paintings from the islands of the South Pacific. Vietnam had the same rustic, primitive feel. There was nothing modern about life in the villages outside the cities. There were no automobiles, no roads, no telephones, no radios, no television, no electric lights, no indoor plumbing, and no architecture that featured glass or concrete. Everything was constructed of bamboo, the furniture, the beds, and the woven mats that composed the walls. All the houses had dirt floors and thatched roofs. In place of streets there was a network of dirt paths that joined with the rice paddy dikes. And the rice paddy dikes themselves were like the membrane walls of a cell. They enclosed an area that flooded with the monsoon rain. This allowed for the rice to be planted. Out in the country, Vietnam was not that far removed from the Stone Age. The villages, and the rice paddies, had a timeless quality that made them beautiful. And the life of a rice farmer was an adventure in simplicity. Everything depended on their hard work, and their direct connection to Mother Nature.

But with the war, everything went straight to hell. Fear distorted our perception. We only saw the danger of a VC ambush coming from the tree lines, and the threat of booby traps in picturesque villages. And, with the passage of time, we saw the Vietnamese themselves as our enemies. We never, not even once, made a friendly connection to the natives. They didn't trust us. And we never trusted them. We were perpetual strangers. Their stoic demeanor held us at a distance. We never understood them. Looking into the face of a Vietnamese villager was like staring at a blank wall. We were just the latest invaders. We replaced the Chinese, the Japanese, and the French. Vietnam had been at war for decades when we first arrived. War had become an integral part of their culture. A rice farmer might be working his paddies while a deadly firefight was going on just hundreds of meters away. It was absurd.

And trying to save the Vietnamese from the communists was even more absurd. They didn't want to be saved. They just wanted to plant and harvest their rice. They wanted to live in peace. They didn't want to die in a war that was fought to establish a western style democracy, which I don't think the villagers ever understood, or cared about. Democracy had nothing at all to offer to a rice farmer. The war was being fought over a lot of political bullshit that would eventually pass away. It was like a vicious storm, or a high fever that needed to burn itself out. In the meantime, a lot of people would be horribly injured, and too many would die a violent death.

When we came to Vietnam we were hyped up on American political propaganda, and unrealistic idealism. We thought we were invincible. We thought we would beat Charlie, and save South Vietnam, in just a few months. We thought we'd do the job, and that we would be home in time for Christmas. We were like children's balloons puffed up with hot air. Little did we know that Secretary of Defense Robert McNamara, knew by December of 1965, that we would never win. That eventually, Charlie was going to unite his country. Of course, McNamara never said so publically. Instead, he remained silent. He let thousands of soldiers, sailors, airmen, and Marines die in order to remain loyal to his boss: LBJ. In essence, he played us for suckers. All of our actions, all of the deaths, all of the wounded, were in vain. McNamara, the statistician, knew the probability of defeat was very high. The best strategy he could come up with was a war of attrition…which is no strategy at all. So, Vietnam rapidly became a war based on numbers. Instead of taking and holding ground, we counted the bodies of dead VC. And the higher the body count, the greater the victory. It was a mindless, misdirected, and ineffective measure of progress. We never controlled the countryside or the people. And how can you win a war without controlling the land the war is being fought on? We conducted search and destroy operations in an attempt to locate and destroy the enemy. That was the best we could do. In effect, we let the VC control the countryside. We came into an area, confronted the VC, and when the battle was over, we pulled out. And after we left, the VC would move back into the same area. All we wanted was a body count that suggested we were killing them at a higher ratio than they were killing us. It was a game of death. The Marines were supposed to have a kill ratio of 10 to 1. But I think that was overly optimistic bullshit. Commanders inflated their numbers to make themselves look good. They wanted to be promoted. They wanted to win medals. They wanted to be admired. So they lied. They made up numbers. After a fire fight, they'd just assume that so many VC had been killed. Statistics turned the war into a series of random clashes that could only be defined by subjective probabilities. What was the chance that we'd be ambushed if we chose to take a specific path while we were on patrol? What was the chance that someone would step on a booby trap as they entered a village? What was the chance that our own FO would call in artillery on us by mistake…as happened several times. What was the chance of being shot in the head and killed? What was the chance of being wounded? What was the chance that we'd survive the war and go home in one piece? We couldn't say with certainty. Vietnam was a war defined by vague probabilities that were nerve wracking in the extreme. We did our best to handle the fear that rose from our uncertainty. We concentrated on living our lives in the moment. That was all we had. The past and the future were full of death. So we tried to enjoy sipping from a cup of C-ration coffee, smoking a cigarette, looking at the sunset, or talking and joking around with our buddies. Confronted with our situation, I feel fairly certain that a majority of the guys in my platoon felt like they were going to die. There was a hopelessness, which we never talked about, which nonetheless pervaded our secret thoughts. Our lives had been given over to an impersonal force that was bigger than any individual. I mean the war itself, which had a momentum that was fueled by death and destruction. It was like being caught up in the churning mass of a giant Tsunami as it broke and washed everyone and everything away. We had to give into it. There was no other choice. In fact, we were part of the wave. There was no separation between us and the violence, the deliberate hunting and killing of our enemy.

I think we also wanted our suffering to matter. We didn't want to suffer and die in vain. We needed a cause that we could use to justify our sacrifice. But all we had was empty propaganda and political scare tactics. Did anyone want to lose a leg, or to give their life to prevent a row of dominoes from tipping over? Did anyone really believe that we were preventing the communists from coming ashore in California? It was absurd. The entire war was absurd. As time passed, killing became its own justification for the war. It had no reason other than self-defense. There was no higher purpose that we could believe in. Defending democracy in South Vietnam was a ridiculous joke. South Vietnam never had a democracy. It was ruled by autocratic generals who were corrupt and dishonest. They used the war to get rich, to take care of themselves. They rigged elections, and they didn't give a damn about the people. And so, on our side, the war became pointless. It turned into war…for the sake of war…killing for the sake of killing.

One time I was sent off on a detail that took several days. When I returned to my company, I discovered that everyone was gone. They were off on a new operation out in the jungle. Our company first sergeant told me to hurry up and get my gear ready. Then I was told to report to the LZ.I was ordered to catch a helicopter that was flying in a load of supplies for my unit. The sky was overcast. It was drizzling rain. I saddled up, put on my poncho, grabbed my rifle, and walked the short distance to the LZ. Ten minutes later I was airborne. I was crammed in among boxes of C-rations, and some five gallon cans of water. I was heading back to the jungle to join my platoon.

The LZ in the jungle was a clearing at the base of a hill. It was easily seen from the air because it was clay that had a brownish red color. The helicopter went into its death spiral, circled around, rapidly lost altitude, and then touched down in the center of the LZ. I jumped off. Then I moved to one side of the LZ to get out of the way of the guys who were unloading the supplies. A few minutes later the chopper lifted back into the air and the LZ was clear. I had no idea what I was supposed to do. I had no idea where my platoon was, or who I was supposed to make contact with. So I just stood around in the rain and did nothing.

Eventually, a sergeant I'd never seen before approached me. He asked me who I was, and what unit I was with. I gave him the information he required. In response, he told me that some guys from my outfit would soon be coming down to pick up their supplies. In the meantime, he asked me to guard a prisoner.

"Where's the prisoner at?" I asked, looking around the LZ. "I don't see anyone who looks like a prisoner."

"He's over there behind the pile," the sergeant said.

"The pile? What pile? I asked. I was confused.

"That pile behind that large stack of C-ration boxes," he said, pointing his index finger. "Just walk over there and you'll see the prisoner. Then you can relieve the guy who's been guarding him."

A few seconds later I headed for the high stack of C-ration boxes. I had no idea what I was getting into. Events in Vietnam always seemed to go from ignorance to surprise and shock in a short period of time. This transition happened when we walked into ambushes. It happened when someone touched off a booby trap. It happened when the local sniper decided to rattle our cage. It happened when Charlie decided to lob some 60mm mortars at our positions. I had no problem with ignorance. It was the surprise and shock that I truly hated.

When I walked around the stack of C-ration boxes I suddenly encountered a large pile of dead men. I stopped. I stared. My mouth fell open. It was unreal. I'd never seen so many dead men in one place. It was unbelievable. They were sprawled on top of one another like jack straws. Some were missing arms and legs. Some had their stomachs blown open. Some had been shot through the head and their brains were leaking out. A few had no discernable wounds at all. There must have been twenty-five of thirty bodies. No doubt this was the pile the sergeant had referred to. After the initial shock had decreased, I became curious. I walked over to the pile and stared at a young man who was lying on his back with his arms spread wide. He was on top of the pile. His head was tilted back. There was a clean bullet wound through his forehead just above his right eye. I couldn't see the exit wound. The rain had washed away his blood. His eyes were closed. There were very few flies. I stared at him for a minute or so. I don't know why. I wanted to turn away, but the mystery of death drew me in. I felt sorry for the young man. I felt sorry for myself. I felt sorry for the country of Vietnam. I realized that I could have been the one lying in that pile. I realized that in killing our enemy, we were also killing ourselves. I had nothing against this dead man. I didn't hate him. We were both caught up in the impersonal, and de-humanizing, machinery of war. Our fate was being decided in another room, and there was nothing we could do about it. How much choice do you actually have when you're caught up in a war and fighting to stay alive? War is a brutal form of monopoly. It simply takes over and your choices are few.

I finally managed to break away. Then I walked around the pile looking for the prisoner. He turned out to be an old man. He was squatting down. His hands were tied together behind his back with com wire. And the com wire was attached to a wooden stake that someone had driven into the earth. I relieved the guy that was guarding him. Then I lit up a cigarette. The old man's eyes followed my every move. But his face had no expression at all. I began to wonder if the old man knew any of the dead men in the pile. I was sure that he did. Maybe several of the dead were his sons? It was impossible to say. There was no trace of grief or sorrow on the old man's face. He just squatted down and watched what I was doing… which was nothing at all. I felt sorry for the old guy. I finally lit up another cigarette and walked over to him. Then I placed the cigarette between his lips. He nodded his head as if to say thanks. There was nothing else I could do.

About ten minutes later I was relieved by another Marine. A squad from my platoon had come to the LZ to pick up our supplies. I joined up with them. They handed me a box of C-rations to carry. Just as I was about to leave the LZ, a chopper approached the pile. After it went into a hover someone on board pushed two bodies out of its side door. They quickly fell into the pile. Then the chopper slowly spun around and flew off. A few moments later, I turned away. I began to follow a muddy path that led up a hill to where my platoon was located. When I arrived, I was glad to see that the guys in my squad were all okay. I wondered if they'd seen the pile of dead bodies in the LZ. I was still trying to come to terms with the experience.

"Did you guys know that there's a large pile of dead bodies in the LZ?" I asked Steve and Jason.

"We saw it yesterday when we first arrived on this hill," Steve replied. "Since then it's probably grown a little bit. Charlie is getting his ass kicked."

"You should have been here two days ago," Jason said. He was drinking a cup full of C-ration coffee. "We got in a firefight that went on for about an hour. They nailed us when we were halfway across a rice paddy. We managed to withdraw under fire. Then we called in artillery and an airstrike."

"Some of those dead gooks were killed in the fire fight," Steve said. "We found a number of dead bodies after we were able to enter the village."

"Was anyone hit?" I asked.

"Second platoon lost a couple of guys who were wounded," Steve said.

"That's too bad," I said. "I'm sorry I missed the fire fight."

"Sure you are," Steve said. Then he began to laugh.

A few moments later I jumped into a nearby foxhole that I would share with Steve. There was six inches of muddy water in its bottom. My feet were already soaked so it didn't matter. In fact, my entire body was wet. Only the top of my head, which was covered by my helmet, was dry.

I wanted to tell Steve about looking at the dead young man. I wanted to share my feelings. But then I decided to let it go. What did it matter? The death of others had become a trivial concern. I was still alive, and the young man in the pile was dead. After we left the area, the villagers would dig a lot of graves. Then they would bury all of the bodies. And the war would go on. More young men would die. More piles would be formed, and more graves would be dug. That was the only certainty in our lives. You could always count on Mister Death to keep everyone busy.

My John Wayne

Marines have a perverse sense of humor. We named our tiny C-ration can opener after John Wayne. I don't know who came up with this strange idea. But it swept through the corps and was accepted by everyone as a funny joke. If you didn't have a can opener, and you needed to borrow one, you'd just ask your buddy for his John Wayne. Your buddy, in turn, would know exactly what you wanted.

A C-ration can opener is a trivial, but necessary device. Obviously, without a can opener you can't open the cans that contain your food. Every pack of C-rations came with one. They were so small that you could carry a dozen of them in your pocket. This tiny can opener was unaggressive, un-heroic, and un-dramatic. It had no resemblance at all to the Hollywood image of John Wayne…which is exactly why we began to call it our John Wayne. This name made sense in a weird sort of way. I think it was a sarcastic way of trivializing John Wayne's Hollywood heroism. He was a famous actor. He was not a warrior. And, in truth, he was anything but heroic. While he made his living playing military characters on the silver screen, he never actually served in the military. During the Second World War, he evaded service because he thought it would have a negative impact on his career. He was a draft dodger. In reality, he was a self-serving actor more interested in making movies, and money, than serving his country.

The tough guy image that he nurtured in the mind of the American public was a Hollywood invention. It was a myth. In truth, I think that John Wayne was a hollow man who needed the Hollywood screen to give him life. In real life, I don't think he ever did anything that was the least bit dangerous, or heroic. And so, we named our C-ration can opener after him. It was also a way of poking fun at all of the Hollywood bullshit. We knew what being a warrior involved. There was no Hollywood bullshit in the firefights we were in. They were as real, as real can be. And I don't think anyone on our side of the game thought of themselves as being a heroic figure. Heroism was a reverential state of mind that we reserved for our dead. Those of us who were still alive survived in a world that oscillated between courage and cowardice. We could be both brave and fearful at the same time. And sometimes courage won the tug o war, and sometimes cowardice took the prize. Whatever the outcome, it was far removed from any movie screen. We were not actors reading from a script. Our dead didn't come back to life after the director yelled cut. Our dead were gone forever. We grieved over them. We felt survivor's guilt. And we shed tears for them. The heroic roles that John Wayne played were nothing but fiction. He turned waging war in the movies into entertainment.

And yet, millions of Americans went to see his movies. And they thought he was a true patriot and a real hero. That's the power of Hollywood. They turn lies into a fictional semblance of the truth. I'm sure there were lots of young men who wanted to walk in his footsteps. And, of course, there were many women who admired him. John Wayne, the tough guy actor, was an American icon. But he was a character who was created out of empty air. Hollywood gave him form on the silver screen. In reality, he had no substance. He had a talent for becoming the character he was supposed to play. His life was a dramatic form of show and tell.

One hot dusty day I was cleaning my rifle and magazines. I was sitting inside a sandbag bunker on my platoon's perimeter. Steve and Jason were nearby talking with each other. It was around ten o'clock in the morning. Everything was still nice and quiet. The local VC sniper had yet to open fire. As I scrubbed my rifle with a toothbrush dipped in oil, I heard Sergeant Howard coming down the line. He was asking for two volunteers. He wanted a couple of men to go back to the battalion area to meet with John Wayne.

"John fucking Wayne?" Steve exclaimed. "You've got to be kidding. Why would I want to meet with John Wayne? What's the fucking point?"

"It might be good for your lousy morale," Sergeant Howard said. "You'd get to meet a man who represents those Americans who support our effort in the war. He's a true patriot. And he wants to meet some real combat Marines…the guys who are actually fighting the war."

"A true patriot?" Jason said. "I think he's a Hollywood bullshit artist. He wants to use us to buoy up his image. He wants to be photographed shaking our hands. It's all about self-serving publicity."

"Think about what you're turning down," Sergeant Howard said. "You'd get to drink a lot of cold beer while you're hanging out at the enlisted men's club."

No thanks," Steve said. "I can't be bribed. I have my principles. I don't want to be exploited."

"I have more important things to do," Jason said.

"Like what?" Sergeant Howard wanted to know. "There's nothing going on. You're sitting around scratching your ass and bullshitting with each other."

"I'm not going to be used in a Hollywood publicity stunt," Jason said. "I have my dignity to think about."

"And what about you Nicholas," Sergeant Howard asked. "What do you think?"

"I like the idea of getting drunk," I said. "But I don't care about meeting John Wayne."

"That's the right attitude," Sergeant Howard said. "Are you volunteering to go?"

"Why not," I replied.

"You're a fucking traitor," Steve said. He was feigning anger.

"You have no dignity," Jason said. "You're a whore squatting for a can of beer."

"It's a sacrifice I'm willing to make," I said.

"A sacrifice?" Jason said. "Getting drunk is a sacrifice?"

"No," I said quickly. "Meeting John Wayne is a sacrifice. It's the price I'm willing to pay in order to drink a few cold beers."

That nobody in my platoon wanted to meet John Wayne came as no surprise. We'd been in combat long enough to know that the war made no sense, and that we were merely fighting to survive our tour of duty. That was the cold reality we faced. We didn't need a famous actor to tell us that our effort was worthwhile. We didn't need a true patriot to inspire us. Our inspiration, most of the time, was provided by our fear of death. Patriots like John Wayne never know what's really going on. They're dreamers. They're flag wavers. They're painfully simplistic in their thinking. And they love sending in the troops to fight and die, while they sit in their easy chairs, and watch the war on TV.

Anyway, me and a guy from Headquarters Company named Don Sullivan, saddled up. Don was a member of a 106mm recoilless rifle unit that was attached to my platoon. About ten minutes later we climbed aboard a truck that was headed for our battalion area.

"How did you get roped into this detail," Don asked.

"I decided it was a good day to drink cold beer and get drunk," I replied. "So I volunteered. If I have to put up with John Wayne's bullshit I'm more than willing. Why are you going to meet him? "

"I'm following orders," he said, unenthusiastically. "As usual, I didn't have a choice. I think I'd rather be filling sandbags."

As we bounced along the dirt road that led to our battalion perimeter, I began to wonder what would happen when Wayne showed up. I supposed that a group of officers, led by our battalion commander, would greet the Duke as he stepped off the chopper. It would be a big deal with lots of handshaking and ass kissing. Cameras would click, and reporters would ask questions. Wayne would be treated like royalty. A few minutes later, he'd be introduced to the 'real combat Marines' who had come out of the boonies to meet him. Then he'd tell us that the Americans back home supported our effort, and they believed we were doing a good job fighting the communists. He'd tell us the war was worthwhile, and that it had to be fought in order to save the world…or some bullshit like that. In truth, I had no idea what would happen. I just wanted to drink a few cold beers on a hot day. I wanted to get drunk. I wanted to forget about the war for a while. If Wayne never showed up that would be fine with me. Cold beer is always good company.

After our truck arrived at our battalion perimeter we jumped off. Then we went looking for the Enlisted Men's Club. That's where we were supposed to meet John Wayne. I'd never visited the club before. What I found was a medium size tent with a dirt floor. There were some simple seats just outside one end of the tent. They were made out of sandbags. There were no tables. I began to wonder how I would go about ordering a beer. I looked inside the tent to see what was going on. I saw a lot of boxes stacked one on top of the other. And then, much to my surprise, I encountered a guy named George Swift. He'd been in my platoon when we first came ashore in the harbor at Danang. After my company was sent south of the airbase, and we began to get shot at, poor George couldn't take it. When the VC opened fire he got down in the fetal position. He wouldn't get up to advance. He wouldn't even raise his head to fire his fire. He was so scared he was completely useless. So, they transferred him out. I didn't know they'd sent him back to the relative safety of the battalion perimeter to work in the Enlisted Men's Club.

"Hey George," I said happily. "It's nice to see you. I was wondering where they'd sent you. Now I know. You're working in the Enlisted men's Club. How are they treating you?"

"Things are better," he said. "I feel much safer. There's no sniper fire in the battalion area."

George was carrying a box. He put it down.

"So how are the guys in the platoon?" He asked. "I miss them from time to time."

"Since you've been gone a few guys have been wounded," I said. "Sergeant White stepped on a booby trap when he walked down a path that went through a hedge. The explosion mangled his right foot. It also took out two other guys. They were bunched up. And we lost our corpsman Doc Andersen. He got shot in the leg. Joey Torio got shot in the shoulder. A couple of guys got sick. Two guys came down with heat prostration. And second and third platoon have had some casualties. A couple of guys got killed. I never knew them."

"That's too bad," George said. "We're taking more and more casualties. I hear about them all the time. The scuttlebutt is not good."

"It seems like everything is going to hell," I said. Then I got down to business. "So how do I order a cold beer?"

"We don't have any cold beer, "he said. "All we have is warm beer. We don't have any refrigeration."

"Okay. How do I order a warm beer?"

"I'll get you one."

Then he went to the far end of the tent. A minute or so later he reappeared and handed me a can of beer.

"What are you guys doing back in the battalion area?" He wondered.

"We're supposed to meet with John Wayne."

"John Wayne is going to visit us?"

"Yes. The one and only."

"That'll be interesting."

"John Wayne wants to meet some real combat Marines."

"Real combat Marines?"

"Yeah…real combat Marines."

George began to laugh and shake his head.

When I arrived at the Enlisted Men's Club it was around twelve o'clock. By two o'clock there was no sight of John Wayne, and no word on when he would arrive. By that time I'd drunk five warm beers. The temperature was near one hundred degrees Fahrenheit. The beer was more hot than warm. I felt like I was going to vomit. I was drunk for the first time in months. I had given up sitting on the sandbag seats. Instead, I favored sitting on the ground with my back propped up against the sandbag seats. Staying close to the earth had become a habit. At around four o'clock someone came by to tell us that John Wayne had decided to fly to Chu Lai. He wouldn't be paying us a visit after all.

After I climbed back aboard our truck for the ride out to my platoon perimeter, I sat next to the tailgate so I could easily vomit overboard without hitting anyone. I was in terrible shape. John Wayne never appeared. He gave us the middle finger and went elsewhere. I actually felt like I'd been let down. The feeling surprised me because I was sure that John Wayne didn't matter. But maybe, if I was more honest with myself, I'd have admitted to being thrilled at the chance to meet a famous actor. But nothing happened. I just got drunk on warm beer. And as I held on to the tailgate of the truck, and streaked the earth with my vomit, I felt like I'd been played for a sucker. I felt like I'd been set up for a loss, which was exactly what the war was all about. In Vietnam, you could never trust your good expectations. You could only trust the ones that were bad. They'd never let you down.

A Firefight

Corporal Jenkins was my new squad leader. I had recently been transferred to the second squad because they were short several men. Things like this happened all the time in my platoon. Guys were shuffled around to fill gaps created by men who had been killed, wounded, or got sick. Corporal Jenkins was new to the grunts. Before coming to us, he'd been a rear echelon motherfucker. I think he was in transportation. We needed a corporal to fill a slot. The Marine Corps was happy to oblige. Unfortunately, Corporal Jenkins didn't know a thing about the infantry. He was an untrained neophyte. He didn't know small unit tactics. He didn't know how to conduct a patrol. He didn't know how to set up an ambush. He didn't know how to avoid booby-traps or sniper fire. He didn't know how to use cover and concealment. And, worst of all, he wouldn't listen to us. He thought he knew everything. He was in charge, and that was the end of the story. We were supposed to follow his orders without question.

On a patrol that passed by the south end of the airstrip at Danang, we came to a large open area. I was walking point. I held up the patrol. Then I sent word back down the line for Corporal Jenkins to come up. I didn't want to enter the open area. I wanted to take a route through a nearby village that would conceal our presence. This was important because there were a number of heavy weapons, including tanks that had been placed at the south end of the airbase. They were on the other side of a mesh fence. Their field of fire was the open area. I didn't want to expose the patrol. I wanted to remain concealed. I absolutely hated crossing open areas. I had been ambushed once before, and I had no desire to repeat the experience. So I whispered for Corporal Jenkins to come up. I wanted to share my plan. Staying concealed was always safer than being exposed. If the VC couldn't see you, obviously, they couldn't shoot you. I was afraid that crossing the large open area might catch the patrol in a crossfire. If some VC sniper opened up, it would trigger a response from the heavy machine guns on the other side of the fence. We would be caught right in the middle with no cover at all.

Corporal Jenkins came up. We whispered to each other.

"I'd like to change the patrol route," I said quietly. "I don't want to walk across that open area. I'd rather go through that village and stay out of sight. I don't want the guys guarding the south end of the airstrip to even see us."

"I don't think that's a good idea," he said. "I think we better fire off a green flare and let them know we're friendly. Then we should head straight across the open area so they can see us."

I didn't agree with him, but there was nothing I could do to change his mind. A minute or so later, I fired off a green flare. Then we headed across the open area. I was very nervous. Without cover or concealment I felt naked. I felt like I was walking across a stage in front of an audience. The open area only covered around an acre, but it seemed to be much larger. Walking point was the most dangerous position in the patrol. It meant that I would be the first one to meet the enemy and, most likely, the first one to be shot.

When we were halfway across the open area, some idiot on the other side of the fence flipped on a search light. Everyone hit the deck. Then the light went off, but not before it ruined our night vision. We got back up. Then we blindly stumbled on our way. There was no shooting. But I was really pissed off at Corporal Jenkins. I thought he endangered the patrol unnecessarily. But I wasn't in charge. He was.

And there wasn't anything I could do. Corporal Jenkins had no fear of open spaces. Strangely enough, I think he believed that he could go on with his life in a normal sort of way, ignoring the reality of combat. This approach would involve no use of cover and concealment for protection. It was idiotic and dangerous. Maybe he didn't think that our enemy was real? A little bit of fear on his part could have changed things for the better. Fear was an important emotion. It could stop you from doing things that were stupid. It could keep you alert. It could keep you quiet when it was necessary. And it could provide lots of adrenalin when the shit hit the fan. Corporal Jenkins was fearless. Only fools and madmen were fearless in Vietnam. And a fearless squad leader could get you killed.

About a month later my platoon was on another patrol and, once again, I was walking point. My Platoon Commander, Lieutenant Dawson, knew that I'd finished an MCI course on map and compass reading. So he trusted me in the point position. I was a good navigator. All he had to do was give me a map with our assigned patrol route drawn on it. I never got lost.

This time we were on a sandy path that ran parallel to a marshy area that had a lot of cattails growing in waist deep water. As we approached an open area, Lieutenant Dawson held up the patrol. He wanted to talk with me about something. Everybody got off the path and took cover…except for Corporal Jenkins. He decided to sit down right out in the open. He really loved being in the open. He leaned back against a dirt embankment and drew up his knees. Maybe he thought he was immortal? Maybe he thought he was invincible? In reality, what he was doing was really stupid. It violated the basic rules. When a patrol comes to a stop everyone is supposed to get down, stay alert, and take cover. As Lieutenant Dawson came up the column, there was a quick series of rifle shots! One, two, three! And that was all. It caught everyone by surprise. We had no idea where the fire had come from. It was loud enough for the shooter to be close by. And it was very accurate. The three shots had taken out three men. Two ARVN troopers that were assigned to my squad were both wounded.

One trooper had been shot in the leg. The other trooper had been shot in the stomach. It was a serious wound. And Corporal Jenkins had been shot through his crotch and was in terrible pain. The VC sniper was an excellent shot. We had absolutely no idea where he was. Everyone waited for another shot. We were hoping to see a muzzle flash. But it didn't happen. There was nothing but nerve wracking silence. The damage had been done.

A few minutes later, Lieutenant Dawson ordered us to form a skirmish line and to sweep into the cattails. I guess he thought the sniper was hiding in the waist deep water of the marsh. So we waded in. I fully expected the sniper to pop out of the water like a Jack in the Box, aim his rifle, and shoot me in the head. But nothing happened. So everyone waded back to dry land, and knelt back down. Our defense was futile. We really didn't know what we were doing. The sniper was playing us for fools.

The open area that Corporal Jenkins had been resting in when he was shot was large enough for an LZ. So we set in a perimeter, and Lieutenant Dawson, called in for a medevac. Our Corpsman Doc White, treated the wounded with morphine to kill their pain. Then he bandaged them up. Corporal Jenkins was out of it. He lost consciousness. His trousers had been pulled down. Doc White covered his bullet wound with a large bandage that resembled a diaper. Corporal Jenkins was a big guy. Dressed up in his bandage I thought he looked a little bit like Baby Huey, the cartoon character.

We heard the medevac approaching the LZ about ten minutes later. Someone threw out a red smoke grenade to mark the center of our perimeter. In fairly short order, the chopper came in for a landing. After the dust settled, the ARVN who had been shot through the leg limped out using his rifle as a crutch and climbed aboard the chopper. Then a group of four guys carried the other ARVN to the chopper and placed him aboard. Finally, four more guys carried Corporal Jenkins to the chopper and tried to load him aboard. They got his feet through the door, but they were having trouble lifting his butt up high enough to slide him in all the way. Corporal Jenkins was out of it. I don't think he even knew what was going on. His body was limp. As the four guys struggled to get him aboard the chopper, the sniper opened fire once again. This time he shot at the cockpit of the chopper. He was trying to kill the pilot. He put a hole in the windshield and scared the shit out of the crew. In response, they decided to abandon the LZ. They increased pitch on the rotors and the chopper began to lift back into the air. Unfortunately, Corporal Jenkins hadn't been loaded aboard. He was half in, and half out of the door. As the chopper became airborne, the four guys struggling to get him aboard let go of him. A moment later Corporal Jenkins fell about six feet. He hit the ground hard. The four guys then dragged him out of the LZ. And, once again, nobody had seen the sniper. We still had no idea where he was.

As I kneeled down in my position an ARVN trooper rushed over to me. He was all excited. He was speaking in Vietnamese and pointing at something. It took me a few seconds to understand what he was trying to tell me. When I followed his gestures, I saw a guy sitting atop the roof of his house in a small village that was about three hundred meters away. He didn't have a weapon. I thought the guy was a curious villager trying to see what was going on. Before I could stop him, the ARVN leveled his rifle and took aim. Then he fired three quick rounds. The first tracer hit the thatch of the roof. The second tracer followed the first. The third tracer hit the guy in the chest and knocked him over backwards. I saw his legs disappear over the peak of the roof as he slid down the far side. The first and second tracers set the roof on fire. I didn't know what to say. It was unreal.

In a short period of time, the roof the guy had been sitting on was burning brightly, and fiery hot cinders began floating through the air. They came to rest on the roofs of several other houses that were close by. Then those roofs began to burn. Twenty minutes later it looked like the whole village was on fire. Lieutenant Dawson asked me what happened. He wanted to know why the ARVN had opened fire. So I told him what I'd just seen. When I was finished, he shook his head and just walked away. I think he was far more interested in taking care of our wounded. Corporal Jenkins still needed to be loaded aboard the medevac chopper, which was circling around high overhead.

Lieutenant Dawson finally decided to call in the medevac chopper…again. We didn't know if the area was secure. There was an excellent chance the sniper was still patiently waiting for the chopper to land so he could open fire once again. But we had to take the chance. Corporal Jenkins needed medical care. There was no time to waste. So the chopper came down from on high, approached the LZ, and then touched down. This time six guys carried Corporal Jenkins out to the chopper and quickly loaded him aboard. In less than fifteen seconds, the chopper was airborne, and headed for our field hospital. The sniper didn't shoot. Apparently, he'd called it a day. Not long after the chopper flew off, we got up and continued on our way. We still had a long way to go before the sun went down on another day in Vietnam.

Wolves and Sheep

When a young man picks up an automatic weapon, and puts on a uniform, everything changes. The young man ceases to be a docile sheep. He suddenly becomes a dangerous wolf. He becomes a predator capable of using the weapon to kill other human beings. And he is fully aware of his power…and the greater power of his military unit. In fact, the sensation of power consumes his mind. It changes his personality. He will become more aggressive and, under the right set of circumstances, he can become a cold blooded killer. The weapon becomes an extension of his body. He can point the rifle as easily as you point your index finger. And if he pulls the trigger, the rifle will fire a bullet that can easily take a life. It's this absolute power over life and death that is so mesmerizing. And only the possession of a deadly weapon can produce this result.

Power substantiates the existence of one human being by nullifying the power of another. It's a game that humanity has been playing for thousands of years. Waging war is not an aberration. It's the essence of our human history.

We boarded our choppers early in the morning. As usual, I didn't know where we were headed. Scuttlebutt said we were going on a hammer and anvil operation. My unit was going to play the part of the anvil. This is a simple type of operation whereby several units, usually platoons, or companies, are ordered to sweep the enemy toward the static position of several other units. Metaphorically, it's like a hammer striking the anvil.

On the flight into our position on a hill, we passed directly over another hill that had a trench line. The two hills were separated by a small rice paddy. The hills were neither big, nor high. As we passed over the trench line, we received small arms fire. It sounded like popcorn going off. The door gunner threw out a red smoke grenade to warn the choppers behind us. Then he opened fire. From my seat inside the chopper I couldn't see what he was shooting at, which increased my anxiety to a level near panic. All I wanted to do was to get off that chopper, find cover, and return fire. I felt helpless sitting in the cabin listening to bullets snap through the chopper's aluminum fuselage. Luckily, nobody was hit, and the chopper was undamaged.

As things turned out, my platoon's LZ was the rocky hill that had no trench line. It had no cover that was worth a damn. Nonetheless, we jumped off, and quickly set in a defensive perimeter. The VC that had been shooting at us pulled their usual vanishing act. They quickly vacated the hill with the trench. Somebody said they disappeared into a nearby tree line. After the last chopper left, the place was eerily quiet. The hill my platoon was on was so rocky that we couldn't dig in. We were sitting ducks. I envied the men in our sister platoon. They were set in on the other hill. They had a nice deep trench to hide in. The only good thing this operation had going for it was the fact that we wouldn't be humping day after day…we'd be sitting on our asses waiting for the VC to show up. At least that was the theory. I was very unenthusiastic about future outcomes. I thought we were wasting our time. The VC were anything but stupid. I felt quite sure they had already flown the coop. The moment they heard the sound of incoming choppers they headed for the jungle. It wasn't that far away. I'm sure they had escape routes in place and ready to use. With luck, we'd just sit on our rocky hill, screw around, drink C-ration coffee, and gaze out at the surrounding countryside.

The hammer part of the operation was composed of our sister company. It was scheduled to sweep through a series of small villages that lay in a beautiful green valley. From the way the trees lined up in the valley, I thought there was probably a creek flowing down between the hills that rose up on either side. From our position we could see into the valley. It was several miles away.

That evening I was ordered to take my fire team down to the base of the hill on a listening post. While it was still daylight, I surveyed the area we were going to set up in. There was a small ramshackle structure that stood at the edge of a big rice paddy. I thought it was a storage shed of some sort. Otherwise, there was no real cover to be found. We would have to set up our LP in a wide open area. It was risky to say the least. Our only cover would be the darkness of the night itself.

After the sun sank down, and the stars appeared, me, and Steve, and Jason, passed through our line. Then we slowly made our way down the hill toward the big rice paddy. There was no moon. It was very, very dark. There was no talking out loud…just occasional whispers. We tried to move as quietly as possible. I figured we'd set up somewhere near the shack…for lack of any better place. Then we'd stay on one hundred percent alert for the entire night. There'd be no talking, and no moving around. I had a radio. I would communicate with our platoon commander by keying the talk button. When you did this the radio would hiss. If you keyed once it meant everything was okay. Twice meant trouble was on the way. You were expected to key the radio once every hour, unless there was a problem.

After we set in, we sat in the darkness and waited, and waited, and waited. Nothing happened…which was okay with me. The war in Vietnam taught me to love boredom.

Steve was on my right, and Jason was on my left. We sat shoulder to shoulder about two feet apart. Around two o'clock in the morning I heard Steve whisper.

"I hear something. I think there's someone moving," he whispered.

I listened hard to see if I could hear the noise he was talking about. I came up with a blank. Either his imagination was running wild, or he really did hear something.

"I heard it again," he whispered. "I know there's something out there."

Then, before I could do or say anything, Steve got up. This was not in the game plan.

"What are you doing?" I whispered. "Sit down."

"I'm going to check out that noise," he whispered back.

"No you're not," I whispered urgently. "Sit down. You're giving our position away."

"Don't worry," he whispered. "I'm not going very far."

Then he walked away. It was so dark I could barely see him as he disappeared into the night. I waited. There was nothing else I could do. Steve was really pissing me off. What he was doing was endangering Jason and me. Our only defense against the VC was invisibility. Steve was giving us away.

Several minutes after he left the LP all hell broke loose. Steve had entered the shack that was nearby. Then he opened fire. Tracers flew through the walls and roof. He was really shooting the place up. A few moments after his initial burst of gunfire I caught a shadowy glimpse of Steve as he ran by. Close behind him was a huge water buffalo. Steve pointed his rifle at the buffalo and pulled the trigger. He was running forward, and shooting backwards. The buffalo dropped in place, rolled on its side, kicked its hooves a number of times, and then it died. In the meantime, one of Steve's tracers had started a fire in the roof of the shack. And, in just a few minutes, it was blazing away. I was dumbfounded. I didn't know what to say. Our LP had been totally compromised. Then I heard Lieutenant Dawson calling to me as he walked down from the hill.

"What's going on," he wanted to know, as he approached our position.

"Sir," I said. "Steve shot a water buffalo. And one of his tracers set the roof of that shack on fire."

"I shot two water buffalo Sir," Steve said quietly. "There's another one inside of the shack."

I could have strangled him on the spot. He really made our fire team look incompetent and downright stupid. If he had followed my orders the whole dramatic episode could have been avoided. All we had to do was sit quietly in place and let the night go by.

"Go on back up the hill," Lieutenant Dawson said. "There's nothing else to be done."

"Yes sir," I said. I was disgusted.

And that was the end of the affair. However, the shack burned for most of the night. And the water buffalo that was inside the shack began to cook. It smelled like someone was grilling a steak. Some of my fellow Marines thought it was funny.

"It makes me want to break out the steak sauce," one guy said. "It smells delicious."

"It's making me homesick," another guy said. "It makes me think about a Sunday afternoon barbeque in the backyard."

We spent the rest of the morning doing nothing important. We walked around, smoked cigarettes, drank C-ration coffee, and spent our time bullshitting with each other. Then everything changed. Word came down the line that the beautiful valley was going to be hit by a B 52 arc light operation. Our commanders wanted the valley bombed into oblivion before our sister company began its sweep. Maybe ten minutes later we spotted two B 52s. They were tiny, silvery specks in the blue morning sky. A moment later the valley began to explode. It was a truly awesome display of power. Shock waves sweep into the sky hundreds of feet. They quivered the air and seemed to brush it aside. Rolling clouds of dust obscured the valley. I don't know how many bombs fell, but it was more than enough to completely destroy those villages. After the operation was over, and the dust began to settle, we could see that the beautiful green valley had been utterly transformed. It was no longer green. It was the color of gray dust. It was the color of death.

By early that afternoon, our sister company had begun to sweep down the valley. We sat and waited to see if any VC emerged. Not surprisingly, the VC had decided not to play our game. The sweep was a total bust. There was no enemy contact. Word came down that the next morning we would be lifted back to our regular platoon perimeter. We thought we could relax. But that wasn't true. You could never relax in Vietnam. It was a country that was full of bad surprises.

Early in the morning I woke to the sharp sound of small arms fire. I was off watch. Coming awake took a few seconds. I was confused and disoriented. When I finally came to my senses, I sat up and looked out into the dark. What I saw immediately set me on edge. Adrenalin surged through my blood. It made my heart pound so strong I could hear it in my ears. Tracers were flying off in every direction about two hundred meters to our front. There was a hell of a firefight going on. Then I heard the sound of hand grenades exploding. I had no idea who was involved in the firefight. But whoever it was, they were in trouble. With the amount of small arms fire that was going on, I figured somebody was being killed. A few minutes later the word to move out came down the line. My platoon was going to cross over to the hill with the trench line. And the platoon that currently occupied the trench was going to rescue the unit that was involved in the fire fight. We quickly saddled up and got underway. The thought of vacating our rocky, barren hill for one with a trench line was very appealing. With all the shooting that was going on, I really liked the idea of being able to take cover in Mother Earth. The war in Vietnam taught me to love Mother Earth.

We made the short journey across a small rice paddy. Then we climbed up the hill and settled into the trench. Nobody was shooting at my platoon. We were only nervous spectators. But the shooting two hundred meters to our front continued for quite a long time. It was very rare for the VC to hang around after they opened fire. They were smart enough to know that we'd call in artillery and mortars at the very least. So they usually played it safe and caught a hat.

After another fifteen minutes or so the small arms fire finally began to decrease. In its wake, artillery flares continued to pop off in the night sky providing visibility. They made a creepy sound as their parachutes slowly descended to earth. After the shooting stopped, my adrenalin supply decreased, and my heart stopped racing. This was a pattern that stayed with me for my entire tour of duty. I oscillated between extreme excitement, and nervous anticipation. Adrenalin ruled my young life.

We stayed on a one hundred percent watch for the rest of the night. Nobody in my platoon knew who had been hit, or how many casualties they had. I was sure we had taken some casualties. But I was wrong. Later that day, after we returned to our permanent base, I found out what happened. A four man fire team led by Corporal John Legette, had been walking down a narrow path on patrol. He told me that he came to a dark shape lying across the path. He thought it was a dead dog so he stepped over it. The other three guys in the patrol did the same thing. Then, as they moved forward, they discovered four 60mm mortars set up on their bipods. Next to the mortars were stacks of ammo. Corporal Legette stopped in his tracks. When he looked around, he saw a whole bunch of other dark shapes lying on the ground. Suddenly, he realized that he was inside the defensive perimeter of a VC mortar platoon, and that all of the VC were sound asleep. So Corporal Legette, and the rest of his fire team, simply opened fire. They attack from the inside out, rather than the outside in. They just started shooting the VC, one by one, as they lay sleeping. The loud sound of gunfire woke the VC up. All in a panic, the ones that hadn't been shot, ran off into the night. Then they tried to launch a counterattack. That's what the prolonged shooting had been all about. Corporal Legette, and his fire team, held them off until help arrived. Incredibly, they took no casualties, and they killed nine VC. They also capture four mortars that were aimed at the rocky hill my platoon had been sitting on. Corporal Legette was very lucky. And so were the men in my platoon. If the VC had hit us with a mortar barrage it would have been a massacre because we had no foxholes to hide in. We were fully exposed.

This was one of the strangest firefights I ever saw. I deeply admired Corporal Legette's suicidal courage. If I had been in his position I'm not really sure what I would have done. He was, so to speak, surrounded by the enemy…even though they were fast asleep. The fighting had been at point blank range. I would never have guessed that four Marines could take on a platoon of VC, and come out of the fight with no casualties. It was an amazing outcome.

Corporal Legette was awarded the Navy Cross, and the three men in his fire team received Silver Stars.

Praying to Buddha

I suffered. The guys in my platoon suffered. Our enemy suffered. The people of Vietnam suffered. Even the land suffered. And all the suffering validated our miserable existence. I suffer…therefore I am. It punched our ticket. It rubber stamped our fate. It was indisputable. From one day to the next it was all consuming and irrefutable. And the reason we suffered was because of endless fear and uncertainty. Nobody wanted to die a violent, impersonal death. Nobody wanted to be shot in the head by an enemy sniper. Nobody wanted to trip a booby-trapped Howitzer round that would blow off your arms and legs. And what would your death amount to in the overall scheme of things? If you died in combat it wouldn't change anything for the better. There was always some new guy to fill the vacant slot. And the war would just go on, and on. It was utterly senseless.

General Westmoreland said that he could see a light at the end of the tunnel. I think he was delusional. There was only the tunnel, dark, grim, hopeless, and deadly. We were lost in it. As we groped our way forward we tried to rationalize our suffering. We tried to give it a meaning. The best our incompetent commanders could do was to pretend that we were making progress, that we were destroying the enemy, that we would soon kill so many of them that they would be unable to attack us. We were supposed to win the war because their dead bodies would outnumber ours. I think that was the general idea. But it wasn't working worth a damn.

When Defense Secretary McNamara did his arithmetic he got it wrong. I suspect the outcome was heavily biased in favor of political considerations. I think he fudged his numbers to kiss the president's ass…at our expense. McNamara had been the CEO of Ford Motors. No doubt, the decisions he made on a daily basis were backed up by numbers. Total revenue, profit, sales, costs, and production were all accurately quantized. The numbers were accurate because McNamara was producing cars that didn't bleed and die, that made their way down the production line with machine perfection. As CEO his world was defined by numbers that gave him reliable information. Those numbers defined the state of the company's economic reality. In Vietnam, numbers were useless. There was no production line that was machine perfect. In fact, from one day to the next, everything went to hell. From one moment to the next, everything was unpredictable. McNamara was naïve in assuming that men behaved like cars on a production line.

In the meantime…everyone suffered.

For example, we knew we were going to be hit the moment we stepped into the rice paddy on line, and we began to advance. The water was only ankle deep. It was warm and slushy from mud. The rice crop was close to maturity. It would soon be harvested. The rice paddy was about three hundred meters wide. I could see a tree line on the far side that defined the edge of a village. I knew there was a group of VC hidden in that tree line. I could feel them in my bones. Their weapons were aimed at us. It was just a question of how close they'd let us get before they opened fire. I felt certain of that. I could feel an enemy rifle aimed at my forehead. As usual, I felt like I was wading toward my death one slippery step at a time.

Lucky for us, the VC opened fire when we were only ten or fifteen meters into the rice paddy. They were nervous. They didn't want us to get close. They thought that distance gave them an advantage. It was a mistake. Instead of advancing further into the rice paddy, we pulled back to the tree line we'd just left. Then we got down and returned fire. Nobody was hit. The VC were doing a lousy job. Our artillery forward observer immediately got on the radio and called for support. After he was able to adjust fire, he called in a barrage. It was right on target. The shooting stopped. The fire fight was over. Everyone on our side was okay. We left no one floating face down in the rice paddy.

Instead of going back into the rice paddy, our CO called for choppers to lift us to a hill that overlooked the village. It took some time to carry out the operation. When it was over, we were deployed on a hard rocky hill that rose from a narrow valley just off to the west. The valley ran north and south. To the east we could look down on the enemy village. Then we did nothing for three long days. We sat around in the hot tropical sun and tried to relax. There was no shade. The temperature was over a hundred. The hill was too hard and rocky to dig in. I worried about an enemy mortar barrage. Luckily, that never happened.

Finally, on the morning of the fourth day, my platoon was sent down into the enemy village to check things out. I think our CO wanted to know if the artillery barrage had killed any VC. We formed a column and made our way down the hill. When we were within a hundred meters of the village we got on line. Then we prepared to sweep forward. My fire team was on the right flank of the skirmish line. And I was on the right flank of my fire team. Beyond me there was nothing but a sparse tree line, and another big rice paddy. And across the rice paddy was another village about five hundred meters away. As we slowly moved forward into the village we were on full alert. We didn't know if the VC were still there. As I moved forward I suddenly caught a glimpse of a VC soldier silhouetted inside a large bush. I hit the ground and opened fire. When the VC didn't respond I became suspicious. I stood up and advanced forward. As I approached the bush, I heard zillions of flies buzzing around. The VC had already been killed in the firefight we were in three days earlier. He was propped up in his spider hole. He was cradling a Thompson submachine gun. Twenty or so feet away were the additional bodies of three other VC. There was a still smoking crater from an artillery round in the center of their group. Their bodies had turned various shades of blue and purple, and they were swollen from internal gasses. They were already beginning to rot back into nature. Ants crawled all over them. Flies were buzzing. The smell of death permeated the air. It was a sickly sweet smell, like rotting pork, or chicken. Steve had been next to me in the line. When I opened fire on the dead VC he had rushed over to give me some cover. He began to laugh when he realized the VC was already dead.

"Looks like you killed that poor motherfucker twice," he said. "Maybe he's twice as dead."

"Once should be enough for anyone" Jason said. He had also come over to see what was going on.

"Looks like you found the mother lode," Steve said. He was referring to the three other dead bodies.

"Jesus," Jason said. "That artillery really packed a punch. Those guys didn't stand a chance."

"Let's move forward," Steve said. "Let's get out of here before we're ordered to take the packs and web gear off the dead VC. I have no desire to touch their rotten bodies."

It was a good idea. So we pushed forward toward the far end of the village. The air was cleaner. And we had a nice view of the same rice paddy we had entered three days earlier. Then we held up, got down, and we waited. At the edge of the village, inside the tree line, there were a number of spider holes dug by the VC. They were all fresh. The village had definitely been controlled by the VC. I began to wonder about the presence of mines and booby traps. I felt certain the VC had rigged up as many as possible. The guys in my platoon, who were just walking around, were taking a terrible risk. I reminded Steve and Jason to avoid walking on any path. I told them to play it safe and take to the weeds. But as things turned out, I was wrong. Nobody won the booby prize. Nobody was mangled by a booby trap.

After every artillery barrage, there was likely to be at least one of our shells that was a dud. The VC would recover the unexploded shells, attach some kind of detonator, and then bury it in a place where we were likely to step on it. Where a path narrowed to go through a hedge was always a good spot. Or, they might place it on a path that ran between the rice paddies. In spite of the risk, we would choose the path over wading through the paddy. The VC were incredibly inventive when it came to producing lethal booby-traps. In fact, about sixty percent of our casualties were from anti-personnel mines and various kinds of booby-traps.

We held our position for about a half hour. Then the order to burn the village was given. I knew it would happen. It was entirely predictable. Within twenty minutes there were a number of vacant homes that were lost to flames and smoke. Because all of the homes were constructed from plant material, primarily bamboo and thatch, they were easy to burn. It was not a large village. There were only five or so homes, and a few adjacent structures. Everything was set on fire with the exception of one home that was located in the middle of the village. That home was spared because there was an old Vietnamese woman who had refused to leave. She was kneeling before a simple altar that was located on a wall inside her home. She was praying and chanting to Lord Buddha. She was obviously terrified. A small group of men stood at the entrance to her home and watched what she was doing. Nobody had the heart to torch her house. The old woman just went on with her prayers. She didn't even turn to look at the men who were staring at her in disbelief. This went on for about five minutes or so before it caught the eye of Lieutenant Dawson.

"What's going on," he asked. "Why isn't this house in flames?"

"Sir," someone said, "there's an old woman inside and she's praying to the Buddha."

Lieutenant Dawson made his way to the entrance of the house and took a long look.

"My God," he said, "what's she doing here? She should have left the village."

"Sir, what should we do?" Someone asked.

Lieutenant Dawson knew when to give ground. The men were obviously in favor of sparing the old woman's house. He was forced to do the right thing. There was no other choice. He had to act like a compassionate human being, even though it meant violating his orders.

"Leave her alone," he finally said. Then he walked away.

Her prayer had been answered. All the other houses and structures in the village were destroyed.

While the village was being consumed by flames, we got orders to move out. We were going back to our position on the hill that overlooked the village. We began to form up in a column. But then, suddenly, we got small arms fire from a village that was located across another rice paddy. The VC were over six hundred meters away, so their fire wasn't accurate. Nevertheless, we ran toward a tree line at the edge of the village, got down, and then began to shoot back. But I couldn't see any worthwhile targets. I couldn't make out any muzzle flashes. The VC were too far away. So I just aimed at a distant tree line and fired off a few rounds now and then. It was pointless. But I had to do something.

And then, suddenly, everything went straight to hell. Our pointless fire fight turned into a struggle for life itself…with our own artillery. Our forward observer was located on top of the hill behind the village we were in. And he was seriously confused. He thought the VC were located in our position, and that we were located in the far off village that hid the VC. He had everything backwards. When Lieutenant Dawson called in for artillery support the first shell flew over my head. It went off about a hundred feet behind me. I couldn't understand what was going on. The next shell was closer to my position. It flew over my head and went off about fifty feet to my rear. Our forward observer was adjusting fire. And he was doing a terrific job. I thought about the three dead VC. I was terrified I'd come to the same end. It was unreal. I thought I was going to be killed by our own artillery. What a lousy way to go. Finally, I heard another round coming in my direction. An artillery shell, so I discovered, doesn't travel faster than the speed of sound. You can hear them coming. This shell sounded like a freight train. I was sure it was aimed directly at me. I hunkered down. The shell went off in the rice paddy to my direct front, about twenty feet away. It left a wide, deep crater. It blew mud and water up into the air. I knew our forward observer had found his target. His next move would be horrendous. He was about to fire a barrage that would inflict a number of casualties on the men in my platoon. But, luckily, that didn't happen. At the last minute, before disaster struck, Lieutenant Dawson got through on the radio. He ordered the forward observer to cease fire. If Lieutenant Dawson hadn't gotten through, our platoon would have been slaughtered. It would have been a horrible accident.

I'm quite sure the VC were laughing at our incompetence. To better our situation, Lieutenant Dawson had a man with a rocket launcher fire a rocket loaded with white phosphorus to mark the right target. Then, our forward observer adjusted fire once again. When he was on target, he called in for a barrage that put a quick end to the fire fight.

In the aftermath, we were ordered to return to our company position on the hill…which we did. After all the trouble we'd been through I was happy to be in one piece and still sucking air. I decided I was going to relax by heating up a cup full of C-ration coffee, and smoking a cigarette. But just as I sat down, my squad leader, Corporal James, said our CO needed two men to carry air panels out to the end of a ridge line that ran north from the top of our hill. The ridge line was parallel to the valley. I was told that an airstrike was on the way. We had to mark the flight path to the target with air panels. They were going to strafe the village that had been the source of the small arms fire. Steve and I were selected for the job because we were the two tallest guys in our platoon. This meant that we could hold the bright red air panels nice and high so that they were easy for the pilots to see. The air panels were made out of cloth. They were about three feet, by three feet. They were fluorescent red.

"Jesus Christ!" Steve said, as we walked down the ridge. "We'll be lucky if some VC sniper doesn't open fire on us. These fucking air panels will turn us into targets."

As usual, I couldn't disagree with him. After we reached a point where the ridge began to drop off, we stopped, stood, and we waited for the fast movers to make their appearance. Just a few minutes later we saw two F4 Phantoms. They were on their way down the valley. They were headed for the same village we'd just blown up with artillery. We held up the air panels to let the pilots know they were on target. They were flying one behind the other. The lead pilot waggled his wings to let us know that he could see us. As he roared by, he was very close to us. He was also below us by about twenty feet. The guy in the rear seat looked up at us and saluted. Then, a split second later, the pilot opened fire on the village with his twenty millimeter Vulcan cannon. It was devastating. Houses flew apart. Trees were knocked down. A large cloud of dust rose up. When the second Phantom made its run, there was even more devastation. Several minutes later the first Phantom returned, made another pass, and fired a salvo of rockets. The mangled wreckage of the village exploded into oblivion. More dust rose into the air. Then the second Phantom made its run. They were destroying the destruction they had already created. It was pointless. On the third pass the first Phantom dropped bombs, as did the second. And on the forth, and final run, they dropped canisters of napalm. By that time, Steve and I were walking back up the ridge toward our company position. I stopped and turned around to watch the firestorm. The village was gone. It no longer existed. Our part in the drama was over. We helped destroy a small, nameless village located somewhere in the countryside of Vietnam. I wondered if we had killed any VC, or any villagers? Maybe there was another old woman sitting in her house praying to the Lord Buddha. Who knows? And who knew the numbers? Who could tell Secretary McNamara how many people we killed in that village? We never went down to check things out. Nobody cared....

REST AND RELAXATION

Jason and I rented a nice hotel room in Naha, Okinawa. It had a large bath. I filled it up with warm water and climbed in for a long, luxurious soak. After months of living on the edge of oblivion in Vietnam, I was determined to enjoy myself for the next seven days. Because my platoon was located out in the boonies, I had nothing to spend my money on, so I'd saved a lot. Now I was on R and R, and I planned to spend my money on good food, whiskey, and women. I was a hungry young man. For the time being, I was free of death and destruction. I was back among the living. And I was free to indulge myself. I could wear civilian clothes. I could go wherever I wanted. I didn't have to follow orders. I was free of living like an animal in the dirt and mud. And I was almost free of the fear that had become my constant companion. Even though I was out of the war zone, and there was no one shooting at me, residual fear still accompanied my every move. It was a conditioned state of mind. Alcohol was a good way of temporarily putting it to rest. If I was mildly drunk I felt less anxious, and my memories of the war didn't bother me as much. So, after we left the transient barracks, the first thing I did was buy a fifth of whiskey. Then we checked into the hotel.

It felt good to put on a white shirt, a pair of gray slacks, and a sport coat that was dark blue. Free of the military discipline that controlled and ruled my life, I found that everything felt fresh and new. It was as though I was experiencing the world for the first time. Freedom had that effect on me. And while I realized that me and Jason had to eventually return to Vietnam, during our seven days of R and R, we could live life to the full. And that meant that we were going to spend a lot of our time in various bars and restaurants.

I also planned to buy a camera. I wanted to photograph my buddies, as well as the country and people of Vietnam. I wanted to preserve my experience in photos. There was something in the madness that I wanted to save. I didn't want to forget the war. In fact, I didn't think that was even possible. I was sure that my memories would haunt me for the rest of my life. You can only go through combat once in your life, when you are young, and prone to taking risks. After you mature you will always want to play it safe. And your body will not hold up to the stresses and strains, mental or physical, of combat. Actually fighting a war is a young man's game. But it's the old men who give the orders that get so many young men killed.

Anyway, that evening I was dressed up in civilian clothes. And I was fortified by several shots of whiskey. It was time to go looking for a woman. I was obsessed. Finding a woman was the most important part of my R and R. I didn't want to lie around and sleep. I didn't want to go to the movies. I didn't want to do a lot of shopping. I didn't want to listen to the radio or watch TV. I didn't want to do a lot of drinking. I wanted to get laid. I wanted some love in my life…even if it was the impersonal sex you get from a prostitute. I could pretend. I was looking forward to pretending. I was desperate.

After we caught a taxi, we asked the driver to take us to a bar that had a lot of girls. He laughed at us. Then he told us, in broken English, that he would take us to a dive called the Blue Fox. It wasn't far from the hotel we were staying at. We arrived at the bar a few minutes later. And after we paid the taxi driver, and gave him a nice tip, we walked in. The place only had ten or eleven customers. Three were seated at the regular bar, and the rest were seated at tables. It was still fairly early…around seven o'clock. Two of the guys at the bar were dressed in Air Force uniforms. Four of the guys seated at the tables were also wearing uniforms. Two were Marines, and two were Army. They were seated at different tables. And they were talking and laughing with some Japanese women who were bar girls. The rest of the customers were dressed as civilians. Jason and I took a table, rather than a seat at the bar. I stared at the women. They were beautiful. They wore dresses that were slit open from their hips down. You could see their white panties and the sensual curve of their buttocks. They had long flowing hair, and they were very sexy. Bar girls, generally speaking, were not necessarily prostitutes. They only offered conversation. You paid the girls by buying them drinks, which was probably tea rather than alcohol, at elevated prices. And socializing with them inspired you, in turn, to buy drink after drink for yourself. It was a friendly kind of scam. As you sat and talked, you may have optimistically thought that the girls were interested in having sex…and sometimes they were. Like most events in life, it depended on the circumstances. These were working girls trying to survive. They were a big tease. After you spent all of your money, and were fairly drunk, they might suddenly vanish. They'd just leave you twisting in the wind. The bar girls had brains that were like cash registers. It didn't take long for several girls to spot us sitting alone. I guess we looked like a couple of good marks. They came over and sat down beside us.

"You buy me drink?" one of the girls asked in broken English.

"Sure," I said. "Why not? Order whatever you like."

I was already playing their game, but I didn't care. These were the first two women I'd sat next to in months. I was completely under their control. They were so petite and sexy. It was exciting to actually sit beside a small beautiful woman.

"My name is Suziko," the girl beside me said.

"Hello," I said. "My name is Nickolas."

"You Marine?"

"Yes, how did you know?"

"Your head bald."

I laughed.

"You look like light bulb."

I laughed again. Suziko had a good sense of humor.

Jason was sitting next to a girl name Cathiko. I said hello. Then I concentrated on Suziko. After our drinks arrived, I took a few sips, then I talked some more with Suziko. I was interested in everything she had to say.

"Where you station," she wanted to know.

"In Vietnam."

"You fight communist?"

"Yes. We are on R and R."

"What R and R?"

"It means rest and relaxation."

"So you come looking for rest and relax?"

"Yes. And I'm already beginning to relax."

"That's good. You need woman to enjoy yourself."

"Yes. I need a woman to help me spend my money, to have a good time."

"Ah yes. Good time. I'm very good at good time."

"I'll bet you are."

In a fairly short period of time I felt like I was making easy headway with Suziko. I actually began to think that she might be interested in staying with me for my week of R and R. She was obviously an opportunist. Bar girls don't mess around. They get right to the point. They can tell when a man is lonely and horny. In fact, every man who walks into a bar is lonely and horny. The Bar girls are very perceptive. They have to make a living. They have rent to pay, and food to buy. In their own unique way, they are as desperate as the men they deal with. And they are always looking for a way to make their lives easier.

"You want deal?" She asked.

"Yes. I would like to make a deal."

"How much you pay for one week?"

"One hundred dollars?"

"I want one hundred fifty."

"Okay."

"Okay."

Then we shook hands. That's all there was to it. Suziko, a complete stranger, agreed to be my mistress for one week. She was responding to the monetary reality of daily life. And I was responding to basic biology. We were both hungry. She needed money. And I needed sex. I felt very lucky. Destiny was on my side of the tracks…for once.

About thirty minutes later Suziko and I left the Blue Fox. I said goodbye to Jason. I told him that I'd see him back at our hotel room. Then we made our way to a restaurant that was nearby.

"Are you hungry?" I asked Suziko.

"Yes," she said. "I need to eat."

It was a small but good restaurant. We placed our order and then we talked some more. I was really beginning to like Suziko. I think she could sense how I felt.

"No woman in Vietnam for you," she said. "Long time…?"

"Too long," I said, "only in my dreams."

She smiled. Then she reached out and took me by the hand.

"We save each other," she said. "I need money. You need love."

It was a simple transaction that took a minimal amount of time to create. I was kind of surprised that she was so agreeable. I think our deal was inspired by our mutual desperation.

After we finished eating I paid the bill. Then we left the restaurant. I thought I was going to take Suziko to my plush hotel room. I wanted to take a bath with her. But she suddenly changed my plans. She was very insistent. She wanted me to follow her. I finally gave in. But I have to admit, I was a little bit nervous as she led me down a dark alley. I didn't know where we were going. In response, I became somewhat paranoid. I thought she might be setting me up for a robbery. Maybe she was leading me to a place where a group of thugs would knock me out and steal my money. Nevertheless, I followed along. We were holding hands. It was a case of trust versus fear. And I was caught in the middle. Trust eventually won the tug o war.

We finally arrived at an old two story building. We climbed a set of stairs and entered a small apartment that was divided into two rooms. The place was simply furnished. It had an air of poverty and neglect. Some paint was peeling off of the walls. There was an old, dirty carpet on the floor. In one corner there was a stove and a refrigerator near a countertop with a sink. Above the countertop were a few cupboards. The apartment had one window that was fogged and streaked from old age. There were no curtains. I could see a double bed through a doorway that led to the next room. And there were three worn out chairs sitting next to a round table with a vinyl top. There was also a single light bulb in the center of the room dangling from a wire. Someone had put a paper lantern on it. I was also surprised to see an older woman inside the apartment. And there was another surprise that was even more disturbing. There was a child sitting in a crib that was placed against a wall. I guessed the child's age at around three years. The old woman was obviously a babysitter. As things turned out, she was Suziko's mother. When Suziko went to work at the Blue Fox, her mother came over to watch the baby. I soon learned that the baby was a little girl named Tamiko. She was very cute. I suspected that her father was an American. Maybe he was a Marine that Suziko had picked up in some bar.

I initially thought my relationship with Suziko would be simple, direct, and uncomplicated. She would get my money, and I would get laid. But after I entered her apartment everything changed. She had a little baby that needed to be taken care of. She had a mother. She was destitute. She was living from hand to mouth and barely surviving. I could easily see that she needed money. If I'd been a hard-hearted person I would have turned around and walked out. We would have parted as strangers with no bond between us. But that didn't happen. I overruled my desire to leave. My cold practicality was overcome by a bout of warm compassion. I didn't want to get involved…but I just couldn't walk away. I was hooked. It took less than thirty seconds. How could I turn away? Getting laid suddenly seemed to be unimportant. I felt sorry for Suziko, for her baby, for her mother, and for humanity in general. There's so much suffering in this screwed up world. I was sick of it. Vietnam was nothing but suffering. I was trying to get away from it. But there is no escape. Suffering is a mental and physical cage with no door. In every direction you look, you'll find someone suffering. There's no way out. It's our world. You can try and pretend otherwise, but you're just deluding yourself. You can get drunk, do drugs, take up religion, or you can go insane. It won't change the reality of endless suffering.

And so, for the next week I helped Suziko with her child. We went to the market, and I bought lots of diapers and formula. I bought a bunch of toys. I bought Tamiko, and Suziko, some new clothes. I bought a good supply of food. I helped her clean up her apartment. I played with Tamiko. It was a strange way to spend my R and R. And yes, Suziko and I made love. But that wasn't the most important part of my experience. It was something that just happened along the way. It was as natural as breathing. For seven happy days I was a member of her family, and that was more important than sex. It allowed me to do some good things for her. All the months I'd been in Vietnam I'd been doing bad things that left me feeling guilty. Suziko, and her daughter, gave me a chance to atone for my sins. Instead of killing the enemy, I was helping a woman who had to prostitute herself in order to feed her baby. I was doing something positive. It made me feel important. Killing the enemy made me feel like a non-person…like an animal. I not only hated the war…I hated myself.

And the days ticked by. The end of my R and R cast a shadow that revived all of my fears. I didn't want to go back to the brutal insanity of combat. I wanted to stay with Suziko, and Tamiko. They had become my refuge. Taking care of them was an act of love. By comparison, everything about the war was an act that was based in hatred, fear, and anger. I felt like the war was a terrible mistake. I was certain it was going to get worse. More and more Americans were being sent into the country. And more and more people would die. I began to toy with the idea of going AWOL. But, in the end, I decided to go back to my platoon. I decided to rejoin my buddies. They also needed me. And, even though I was filled with doubts and uncertainty about the war, I needed them. I was an inseparable part of my platoon. Nothing could change that. And my platoon was part of my fate. So, at the end of my R and R, I rejoined Jason, and the two of us caught a flight back to hell. Before I left, I gave Suziko as much money as I could. Then I said goodbye. There was nothing else I could do. I would think about her, and Tamiko, for years afterward. I wondered what happened to them. I wondered if they were okay. Knowing her was a touch of life in the midst of death. For seven short days she gave my life a meaning and a purpose.

Boots

My mind was protecting itself from painful events by numbing me to reality. Confronted by the daily threat of violence, and death, my mind was like a castle under siege. My mind pulled up the drawbridge. It restricted my feelings. Fear and anger were the only emotions that got through. Love, joy, compassion, mercy, and empathy were all shut out. These positive emotions were entirely out of context to the brutal nature of combat. Killing other human beings requires an emotional vacancy that is a form of self-protection. My mind didn't want to experience what my physical body was actually doing. It chose to avoid painful trauma by censoring the flow of information. Only a distorted sense of reality got through. The war always seemed to be unreal. It was more dreamlike than actual. There was a mental disconnection that enabled me to follow orders, even when those orders were a clear violation of moral decency. We never took prisoners. We killed wounded VC. This behavior was a mental nightmare. War is a sickness. And all those who fight in a war, and engage in the death of others, without exception, catch the disease. I became numb to the suffering of others. There was too much to deal with. I think I went insane to remain sane. I did crazy things. I crossed a threshold into a different world. And, I suspected that my crossing was irreversible. It was a one way street into emotional suicide.

Combine my extreme mental stress with physical exhaustion, and you get the thousand yard stare. It's a symptom of resignation to fear and terror. It's an obsessive reaction to a reality that is out of control and can't be trusted. I became a lost soul inhabiting a body attached to an automatic rifle. The weapon was my last defense against complete chaos and death. I turned inward because looking at the outer world was too painful. But there was nothing but fear lurking in the back of my mind. It was like a hungry vulture in a cage. And the fear came out through my eyes. I could sit for hours on watch and stare off into nihilistic nothingness.

Everyday news came down the line about casualties. I heard that Doc Watson, who once treated me for a trivial bullet wound, had been shot through the head by a sniper. I heard that Dennis Holden stepped on a booby-trapped mortar round and died. I heard that Luis Martinez had been badly wounded. I heard that Daniel Ostermier had been shot in the leg. I was sure it was only a matter of time before I was seriously wounded or killed. I tried hard to believe that the numbers were working in my favor. I lied to myself to remain functional, to keep from going off the deep end. Maybe I was driven by nothing but stubborn pride, but I wanted to go on fighting. I'm not a quitter or a coward. My fate had a single narrow path.

And my own platoon had taken a number of casualties. Brady Cooper got shot through the shoulder. Robby King was wounded by a toe popper. He lost his right foot. Mark Linden was shot through the chest and died before we could get him on a medevac chopper. Louis Dobsen was badly wounded by a hand grenade attached to a trip wire. The blast took out two other guys. And the list goes on. In 1966 the war was gaining momentum. More and more Marines were engaged in the awful business of trying to kill the enemy. More and more operations were taking place. And more and more men were being wounded and killed.

During one operation we ended up in a defensive perimeter around a busy LZ. Choppers came and went. They were flying in boxes of C-rations, cans of water, and crates of ammo…the essential resources needed to sustain combat operations. Directly in front of our perimeter was another rice paddy. It was full of muddy brown water. It was about two hundred meters wide. Another nameless village rose up beyond the paddy. We had just spent about a week chasing Charlie through the jungle. We were very tired. We hadn't been able to take off our boots. Our feet had been wet for days. We thought our new position was safe and secure. The village was very small, and very quiet. We didn't pay any attention to it. We were happy to find a nice series of foxholes surrounding the LZ. So we just took off our packs and jumped in. We thought we could finally relax. I took off my boots to air out my feet. I also wanted to put on a pair of dry socks. I was trying to avoid coming down with immersion foot. This is a condition caused by a long exposure to water. During World War One it was called trench foot. Tens of thousands of grunts came down with it. When water leeches out the lanolin, the skin becomes brittle and cracks open. It's very painful. It makes walking extremely difficult, or downright impossible. After I took off my boots I let my feet bathe in the sunlight. I wiggled my toes. It felt good to finally let my feet dry out. I was enjoying myself. I took a few sips of coffee from a C-ration can, lit up a cigarette, and from time to time I looked at the distant village. I saw no sign of movement. To my left was an extension of high ground that slowly formed a U-shape that eventually came back on the village. I could see a large path that rose above the rice paddy. It connected the high ground on my left to the village. This path was the only way to get into the village without getting your feet wet in the rice paddy.

A few minutes after I took off my boots, Corporal James came down the line. I could tell by his facial expression that he was about to give us an order. He was all business.

"Lieutenant Dawson wants you to take your fire team and check out that village," he said. "It's your turn to go on patrol. Get your shit together and saddle up."

My boots were still off. It would take several minutes to put them back on and to get ready. Then Platoon Sergeant Howard yelled in our direction.

"Hurry up with that patrol." He said. "Stop wasting time. The lieutenant wants it done now."

"I'm going as fast as I can," I said to Corporal James. "It's gonna take me a couple of minutes."

"Stop fucking around," Platoon Sergeant Howard yelled again. "Get that patrol underway."

"Fuck it," Corporal James said. "I'll take a couple of the new guys out on patrol. You stay here and drink your coffee. It will be good for their experience. This patrol is a piece of cake. It shouldn't take more than an hour."

Then Corporal James quickly organized his patrol. Four new guys had just joined our squad. They'd been in the country for about a week. They didn't know anything. Corporal James was trying to teach these guys how to stay alive. Taking them out on a simple patrol to a small village was a beginning. A minute or so later, they left our perimeter. They were walking on the high ground that U-turned and came back to the village. I soon lost sight of them. I put on my dry socks. Then I put my boots back on.

Steve had been given a fire team of his own. Our squad was down to ten men. There was Corporal James, and three fire teams composed of three men each. Steve's team had one of the new guys. We'd taken so many casualties that our ranks were filled with fucking new guys. It sounds strange, but I tried not to pay any attention to our casualty rate. Men just came and went. Some were wounded. A few were killed. Some got sick. And some were injured. The fact that we had so many new guys was depressing. And, even with all of the new guys, we were still operating below our tactical operational level. For example, there should have been thirteen men in my squad. We only had ten. And the other two squads were no better off. That meant that our platoon was composed of about thirty three men...including the corpsman. Our TO strength should have been around forty.

Anyway, I soon forgot all about the fire team patrol that Corporal James was leading. He was out of sight and mind. I didn't think anything bad would happen. But suddenly, the quiet afternoon was shattered by the loud sound of a big explosion. This was instantly followed by a strong volley of small arms fire that came from the village. The VC were aiming at us as we sat on the perimeter of the LZ. Corporal James' patrol had been ambushed. I saw a plume of dust. But I couldn't see the patrol. And, in the rush to get the patrol underway, our platoon sergeant had failed to give Corporal James a red flare to mark his position. So we had no idea where the patrol actually was. This was incredibly important because it meant that we couldn't return fire for fear of hitting our own men. They could have been in the village. The VC had us dead to rights. The patrol was pinned down somewhere near, or in, the village. And that's all we knew. To make matters worse, the VC suddenly began to shoot 60mm mortars at the choppers sitting in the LZ. There were three or four loud explosions. After the choppers made their escape, the mortar fire fizzled out.

Then Steve and I did something that was incredibly stupid. We rushed into the paddy and splashed down behind the closest dike. The guys in our fire teams followed along and got on line. Our move was based on reflexes alone. Steve was leading the way. He was going to launch a frontal attack across a rice paddy that was two hundred meters wide. He was crazy as hell. Bullets snapped by. The VC were shooting at us. I fully expected the entire platoon to go on the attack. But when I turned to look, everyone was hunkered down in their foxholes. And they were waving and shouting for us to come back. When I looked forward I could see numerous muzzle flashes. Going back suddenly seemed like a very attractive idea. I thought that a frontal assault was suicide. I shouted at Steve to go back. I waved my hand. But he was in a different frame of mind. I could tell that he was beyond following orders. He was operating on gut instinct. And his gut told him to move forward. His gut told him to close with the enemy. He was beyond fear. He was beyond common sense. I thought he was going to die. As I rose up and turned toward the safety of my foxhole, Steve jumped up and ran forward. A moment later, the new guy in his fire team tried to follow his move, but he didn't make it. A bullet hit him in the head. It sounded like someone had smacked a watermelon with a baseball bat. The poor guy's helmet flew off. He went face first into the muddy water. A moment later Doc White ran by, dove into the paddy, and pulled the guys face out of the water to keep him from drowning. Then he began to bandage the guy's head. By that time my fire team had returned to our foxholes. We stayed low. Then Doc White motioned for my fire team to give him a hand. He wanted us to evacuate the guy that had been wounded. We rushed back into the rice paddy. Somebody produced a poncho. Then we quickly rolled the new guy onto the poncho, and we began to drag him out of the rice paddy. The mud was slippery. It was hard going. The poncho filled up with bloody water. The guy was white as a sheet and out cold. I was sure he was bleeding to death. The VC were still shooting at us and we had to duck down several times. Our progress was slow. Finally, after we emerged from the rice paddy, a group of men from the LZ ran over to help. They carried the poor guy away. That was the last I ever saw of him. I never knew his name. He had only been in the country for a week or so.

In the meantime, the VC were still shooting. Steve was still alive and advancing against the VC positions. He was slowly maneuvering forward using the rice paddy dikes as cover. So far into the fight, the men in my platoon hadn't fired a single shot. We were helpless. Steve's suicidal frontal attack to save the lost patrol was our only response. Then, unexpectedly, Platoon Sergeant Howard, and Lieutenant Dawson, jumped out of their foxhole, and began to charge across the rice paddy. I thought their move was completely insane. Our lieutenant had his forty five caliber pistol in hand, and our platoon sergeant was carrying a twelve gauge shotgun. They ran straight ahead. They didn't even bother to zigzag. They were perfect targets. About half-way across a bullet hit our platoon sergeant in the chest. He went down with a splash. Doc White then ran to help, but he got shot in the leg. He too went down. Lieutenant Dawson didn't even slow down. He just ran straight ahead. What was he going to do with a pistol? His move was crazy. We were losing our leaders. Who was going to run the platoon if our lieutenant was killed? It was totally fucking nuts! As I sat in my foxhole and watched, our lieutenant finally got down behind a rice paddy dike when he was about twenty feet from the VC line. He stayed down. The VC shot round after round trying to hit him. Water splashed into the air.

Finally, a machine gunner in our sister platoon had seen enough. He just didn't give a damn about the lost patrol. He opened fire on the tree line hiding the VC. He walked tracers back and forth. They whizzed just over the head of Steve and our lieutenant. The machine gun fire was effective. The VC disappeared. The fight was finally over. Then our lieutenant pumped his fist in the air. The entire platoon rose from its foxholes. We charged forward across the rice paddy. Men dropped out to help our platoon sergeant and our corpsman. When we entered the village we were filled with rage. We immediately torched the few structures in the village. Then guys went looking for underground bunkers. When they found them they tossed in hand grenades. We didn't care who was down in the bunkers. VC or civilians, it didn't matter.

My friend Steve got hit in the face by shrapnel from a hand grenade. I finally got back up with him after the platoon made its grand charge across the rice paddy.

"I'm glad to see that you're still alive, "I said. "You had me wondering. I was sure the VC were going to kill your dumb ass. You're one lucky guy."

He was covered in mud. He had three or four small, bloody holes in his face from the pellets of a hand grenade.

"It's nice to see you to," he said. Then he gave me the bad news. "Corporal James is dead. He triggered a booby trap. I think it was a Howitzer round…but I'm not sure. It blew him to hell. One of our new guys got knocked silly by the concussion."

"Jesus," I said quietly. "What a fucking mess." I couldn't think of anything else to say, so I said nothing at all. I was devastated.

In addition, one of the VC was wounded by machine gun fire. He was left behind by his buddies when they made their fast retreat. I was told that someone shot him in the head. And that another guy cut off his ears.

By that evening we were back in our foxholes and still winding down from the firefight. Everyone was exhausted. There wasn't much talking. We had taken a beating. We were still pissed off. As we sat in our foxholes collecting our wits, we were surprised to see a Huey gunship zoom in on the village. He made a low pass. His door gunner opened fire. That too came as a surprise. What was he shooting at? The gunship circled back around for another pass. This time when the door gunner opened fire, the VC, who had already slipped back into the village, returned fire. The gunship then began to make pass after pass. Machine gun tracers flew up. And machine gun tracers streaked down. The VC, and the gunship pilot, were playing a deadly game that went on for about ten minutes. Then, during one pass, the machine gun tracers that flew up hit the gunship's tail rotor. A moment later the pilot lost control of his aircraft. It twirled around, and around as it descended to earth. It crashed down somewhere behind the village. I don't know what happened to the crew. Hopefully, they were quickly rescued. Strangely enough, nobody said anything. We just watched in silence, as if seeing a gunship shot down in a village we had just taken, after a terrible firefight, was no big deal. It was just business as usual. And we thought that was the end of the story. But, as usual, we were wrong. Around two o'clock in the morning we were ordered to pass back through the village to find the gunship that had been shot down. Then we were going to form a defensive perimeter, so that a larger chopper could take the damaged gunship away. Needless to say, we were overjoyed. I was certain the VC would open fire on us once again as we passed through the village. But, luckily, that didn't happen. Maybe they were sound asleep after a hard day? Without much effort we found the gunship lying on its side in a rice paddy. After some technicians from the air wing got everything ready, the big chopper arrived. It lifted the gunship into the sky and flew away.

In the aftermath of the firefight, my squad had dwindled down to seven men. The next day, a man in my fire team was evacuated with immersion foot. And the day after that, I was evacuated with a case of severe septicemia. At the beginning of the operation we had to climb a steep embankment to clear the LZ. I was grasping at bushes to keep from sliding down. One of the bushes I grabbed had thorns that were about an inch and a half long. The palm of my hand was punctured by one of the thorns. Then it broke off. Over time it became infected. There was a red streak running from my palm to my armpit. Septicemia can be lethal. During World War One, it killed hundreds of thousands of soldiers. Even guys who had mild wounds died. The battalion doctor put me on a chopper with four other Marines that had various wounds. Then they flew us to the division hospital at Chu Lai. Of the four, I was the least wounded. I was still able to walk. I was embarrassed. I had to sit with my hand elevated, as if I was waving at someone. If I lowered my hand it began to throb with pain. I felt ridiculous.

While I recuperated in the hospital I thought about Corporal James. He had been a close friend. I felt guilty about his death. He had taken out a patrol that should have been mine. If my boots hadn't been off, I would have led that patrol. I would have been walking point. To ease my sense of guilt, I tried to blame his death on poor tactics. He had walked the patrol down the elevated path toward the village. He did it to keep from wading across a rice paddy. He must have known the path was an ideal place to bury a booby trap. But he chose to walk down the path anyway. He got lazy. He got lazy and it killed him. I felt terrible. I blamed myself. I felt responsible. If I had taken out that patrol I would have stayed off the path…at least that's what I told myself. Now it was too late. Corporal James was gone forever. I also learned that Sergeant Howard had died of his chest wound. And I never heard anything at all about the new kid that was shot in the head. I don't know if he lived or died.

I was in the hospital for a week. They gave me two penicillin shots a day. And I had to soak my hand in some sort of liquid solution. Eventually, after the Septicemia cleared up, they put me on another chopper to fly back and rejoin my platoon. My time in the hospital was very relaxing. I spent most of my time lying around. They had a good supply of National Geographic Magazines. I hated to leave. But orders are orders.

After I returned to my platoon, a big black corporal named Benson chewed me out. He was our temporary platoon sergeant. He thought I was malingering. He thought I was evacuated for nothing serious, just a small wound in the palm of my hand. He said I was trying to avoid doing my duty. I didn't argue with the idiot. I just tried to ignore him. Then I walked away when he was through with his bullshit. And so…that's how I re-joined my platoon. Steve and Jason were glad to see me. And I was glad to see them. I thought Steve was a hero. I thought they should have given him a medal for his suicidal attack. But, of course, that never happened. The war just went on, and on. And the green machine was grinding meat at an ever faster rate.

Fucking New Guys

I think the new guys who came into our outfit were fighting two wars at the same time. First, they were fighting the VC, which was a very real enemy. Second, they were fighting with an over abundant amount of fear. And their fear was fueling their imaginations. As a result, these new guys had a tendency to be trigger-happy. At night, on the line, a shadowy bush could become a VC sapper. The sound of the wind rustling the leaves of a nearby tree, could sound like the approach of a VC platoon. The new guys hadn't learned the fine art of separating reality from the murky churnings of their overactive imaginations. They hadn't learned to use common sense. Their fear created a confusing state of mind. In essence, they hadn't learned to be at ease with their fear, to keep it in perspective, and to remain calm and cool. To some extent, they had to learn how to distrust what fear could do to their mind and body. They had to learn to see through it. And that took time.

I think a lot of new guys thought that the war was a life and death struggle that went on each hour of the day. But that wasn't true. In fact, the war I fought in 1966, from one day to the next, was mostly nervous boredom. Nothing at all happened. No shots were fired. There were no enemy attacks. There was only sweaty heat, mud, rice paddies, bugs, long tiring patrols, no showers, and crappy food. Firefights were actually fairly rare. They only happened often enough to keep us on edge. It took a while for the new guys to settle down, to realize that overreacting to their fear could be dangerous. In truth, a new guy with an automatic weapon could be more dangerous than a VC sniper. The war had some brutal lessons to teach.

My platoon had been ordered to go on patrol…again. My platoon commander gave me a map with the route sketched in. Then he ordered my fire team to walk point. It promised to be another long, hot, sweaty day. The air was filled with a slight morning haze. I could smell wood burning in cooking stoves. A mild breeze rustled the leaves of the trees. The rice paddies were full of muddy brown water, and new rice plants.

I was still slightly groggy from a night spent on fifty percent watch. I never got enough sleep in Vietnam. From sundown, to sunup, I'd be lucky to get four hours of uninterrupted sleep. If it rained I'd be lucky to get any sleep at all. In any event, as our patrol got underway, I began to wake up. I surveyed my surroundings, and picked the best path forward. Then I told Steve where to go. He was our point man. I was right behind him. Jason was behind me. And our new squad leader, Corporal Baker, was behind Jason.

The patrol was monotonous. The hours seemed to limp by on crutches. We passed through three or four villages without any trouble. There was no sniper fire, or booby traps. The villages all had barking dogs, and children. These were good signs that the VC were absent. When the VC moved into a village, all the people, and their dogs, moved out to avoid trouble. Quiet empty villages were dangerous. If you didn't hear the sound of children laughing and playing, you'd better get ready for trouble.

Around noon we set up a temporary perimeter so we could eat a quick meal of C-rations. I was definitely ready for a break. While our going had been slow and easy, it was still tiring because of nervous anticipation. Walking point was a risky proposition. You had to remain on high alert. You had to use your eyes and ears. You had to pay attention to where you were placing your feet to avoid booby traps. You had to watch out for trip wires. You had to move as quietly as possible. And you had to choose a route that provided good cover. Walking point was the most difficult job in any patrol. And, if you ran into trouble, the point man was the most vulnerable. Most likely, he was the one who would encounter the enemy first. Which meant the chance of being shot and killed was very high. After our brief lunch, we saddled up, and we got underway again. I relieved Steve of his position as point man.

By that evening we were looking for a good place to set in for the night. Luckily, we found a large clearing that was a Buddhist cemetery. At least, I think it was a Buddhist cemetery. But I'm not really sure. It had a number of strange graves. Each one had a circular parapet about ten feet in diameter, and two feet high. There was a smaller mound, about three feet in diameter, in the center of the circle. The graves were made from dirt that had been packed so hard it was almost like concrete. I assumed the corpse was buried under the mound. I also assumed that the circular parapet, which surrounded the mound, had some symbolic significance. Maybe it defined resurgence and rebirth? I didn't know. Anyways, the space between the parapet, and the mound, was deep enough to provide good cover…which meant that we didn't have to dig in. All we had to do was lie down and conform to the circular nature of the grave. The grave's dirt parapet would protect us from small arms fire. So…we moved in. Steve and I would share the grave of a dead Vietnamese. The three of us would spend the night together. It was a strange kind of foxhole to be sure. And yet, it seemed to be compatible. Necessity was creating strange bedfellows. Near sundown we ate another C-ration meal. Then we set the watch. Steve got the first four hour shift. I rolled up in my poncho, took off my helmet to use for a pillow, and then I went to sleep.

I felt someone patting me on my leg. It was Steve. He was waking me up. It took me a minute to come to my senses. I sat up. I wiped my eyes. I put on my helmet. Someone had tossed an illumination grenade out in front of our line. The bright light hurt my eyes.

"What the fuck is going on?" I asked. "Who tossed the grenade?"

"I don't know," Steve said. "Maybe someone heard gooks probing our line?"

That's bullshit," I said. "There's no chance the gooks are probing our line. Someone's imagination is running overtime. I'll bet it's one of the new guys."

"My night vision has gone to hell," Steve said. "I'll be blind as a bat when the grenade burns out."

A short time later the grenade burned itself into darkness…and silence reigned…but not for long. Suddenly, there was a short burst of automatic fire. Tracers flew straight down the line. Steve and I ducked down instinctively. It scared the shit out of us. Then someone began to yell for a ceasefire. They were all upset.

"What the fuck is going on?" Steve asked. His adrenalin was up and he was angry.

We seemed to be caught up in a weird set of circumstances that were out of our control. All we could do was stay in place and watch.

"It's got to be one of the new guys," I said again.

Then we heard someone yell for our corpsman, Doc White, to come up. They sounded like they were close to panic.

"Someone's been shot," I said. "What else could it be? Why else would they yell for the corpsman?"

"Jesus Christ!" Steve said angrily. "This night is turning into a fucking nightmare."

Then I could hear men talking. But their voices were so faint I couldn't hear what they were saying. The darkness, and our loss of night vision, completely obscured whatever was going on. We were left nervously twisting in the wind.

About twenty minutes later, we heard the sound of an approaching chopper. Then I saw a shadowy figure walk out into a nearby clearing. He was carrying a flashlight with a red lens. He pointed the flashlight skyward to pinpoint the LZ for the chopper. I knew it was a medevac. I also knew that someone was seriously injured…maybe even dead. But I didn't know any of the details. I didn't know who had been shot, who did the shooting, or why the shooter had hit one of our own men. It was crazy! Things like this were not supposed to happen.

The chopper made a beautiful pinpoint landing, which was no small feat considering the circumstances. Then, a minute or so later, it lifted back into the sky and flew away. I knew it was carrying a young man who had been shot by his neighbor. I was putting sketchy information together in my tired mind, and I could come to no other conclusion. Someone, probably a new guy, had pulled the trigger on a fellow Marine.

"My God," I said quietly, "this war is just one tragedy after another. There's no fucking end to the bullshit. Just when you think you've seen it all, something new goes to hell."

"Yeah," Steve said. "Vietnam has an endless supply of bad surprises."

By this time, Steve's four hour watch had come to an end. It was now my turn to stare off into the night for hour after hour, until the sun rose at dawn, and filled the land with light for another anxious day.

And I was right. It was a new guy who shot his neighbor. But there's more to the story. The two of them had gone through boot camp together. They were close friends. During the night the guy that did the shooting thought he heard gooks probing our line, so he threw out an illumination grenade. After the grenade burned out, his friend, who was right next door, made the stupid mistake of leaving his position. Maybe he was curious about what was going on. Maybe he wanted to talk. So he ran toward his friend. And his friend mistook his shadowy silhouette for an enemy VC…and shot him down. The shooter was a trigger happy new guy with an overly active imagination. He was hearing and seeing things in the dark. The two of them had been in the country for less than a week. I was shocked and saddened. It was a terrible mistake.

While I was making a cup of C-ration coffee, and smoking my first cigarette of the day, I saw the guy who did the shooting sitting by himself on the edge of the LZ. He was waiting for our supply chopper to fly supplies in, so that he could fly out. He was a total wreck. He felt so bad that he was entirely useless. He held his head in his hands. He stared straight down at the dirt beneath his feet. Guilt and grief radiated from him like light from a table lamp. There was nothing anyone could do or say to cheer him up. And, to be honest, nobody wanted to comfort him. It was better to leave him alone. He fucked up. He lost his cool. He couldn't be trusted. It was better to let him go. He no longer belonged to our platoon.

The trade

One day, as we were standing in formation, my platoon sergeant called for volunteers. He said they were looking for men to attend sniper school. To qualify you had to have shot a score of high expert at the rifle range. I qualified. So I raised my hand. I didn't have any particular desire to be a sniper. But if I had to make a choice between attending school, or going on patrol, I'd choose school. That was a no brainer. He said the school would last about two weeks. That was two weeks of good duty as far as I was concerned. It meant that I wouldn't be standing watch at night so I'd get a good night's sleep. It meant that I'd be sitting on my ass listening to an instructor instead of filling sandbags. It meant that I wouldn't be a target for the local sniper. And it also meant that I'd be learning something new, instead of doing the same old thing day after day.

The school was conducted on the south side of hill 327, which was located to the west of the airbase at Danang. I think it was the first sniper class the Marine Corps ever conducted during the war. Fifteen men from my battalion showed up. Our instructor was an officer named Captain Fletcher. There were only three rifles that were available. So, we had fifteen men who were going to shoot three rifles to qualify as battalion snipers. No doubt there would be a lot of waiting around to take your turn with the rifle. Moreover, only the top three shooters would be given a rifle at the end of the course. We were competitors. I assumed that we were also the best shots in our battalion. Naturally, being Marines, everyone wanted to win a rifle. And the rifles were entirely unique. They were beautiful Winchester Model 70s, with an eight power Unertl scope. Each rifle had a caliber of .306. They also had a heavy barrel, held five rounds, were bolt action, and they had an effective range of around six hundred meters. The scope was sitting on two sliding mounts. These mounts prevented the shock of the recoil from disturbing the crosshairs in the scope. After each shot you had to reach up and pull the scope back into place. Essentially, this rifle was a hopped up version of an ordinary deer rifle. It also had a wooden stock, and a hair trigger. By comparison, the Winchester made my poor old M14 look awkward and clumsy. It was like comparing a thoroughbred to a work horse.

The first few days of the school covered subjects related to the operation of the rifle and its scope. We learned about adjusting its elevation and windage knobs. We were also told how to form a sniper team, how to choose a good position, what time of the day and night to go out and come back, the importance of camouflage, and how to sight in the rifle on your enemy. On that score, we were told to shoot at the center of the body, namely the stomach and chest, not the head. Tactically speaking, a wounded enemy is better than one that is dead. A dead VC can be left alone. A wounded VC will require evacuation and medical treatment. This means that two or three of his comrades will have to expose themselves in order to drag the wounded VC back into cover. And, once they are exposed, they too can be shot. Snipers play a brutal, unforgiving game. They are merciless. And they can be a powerful force on the battlefield. One good sniper can hold up the advance of an entire company. It's also a dangerous occupation. Snipers have a high casualty rate. Nobody likes dealing with snipers.

I listened to everything Captain Fletcher had to say. Having been in Vietnam for many months, I thought that a lot of his information was old hat. But the information about the rifle was new and interesting. For instance, the rifle had a barrel that was heavier than normal. In essence, it had a greater diameter. And this barrel was 'floating', which meant that it didn't touch the stock. There was a thin space between the steel of the barrel and the wood. This made the barrel very accurate. There were no distortions in the energy that flowed down the barrel when the rifle was fired. The rifle was like a very fine, very precise, tool. And, if the scope was properly adjusted, the rifle was highly accurate.

We started shooting around the end of the first week of school. Captain Fletcher had placed fifteen number ten cans at various ranges, from two hundred meters, to six hundred. A number ten can is about the same size as a human head. The cans were tied to a stake in the ground to keep them from flying off when they were hit. Once the scope had been zeroed in, we found that hitting the cans at two hundred meters was easy. The rifle was so accurate I could have hit a playing card, over and over, at that range. As the range increased, the rifle became a little less accurate. If I was able to hit a number ten can five times out of five shots at two hundred meters, I was only able to hit a can three out of five times at six hundred meters. To be sure, six hundred meters is around a third of a mile.

Day after day we practiced shooting. Finally, on the last day of class, we competed with each other to see who would win a rifle. I lucked out. I shot a good series. I hit the six hundred meter can four out of five times. So I won a rifle. I was very happy with my new toy. I felt like a hot shot. My head got big. My ego swelled up. I thought I was special. I thought I was a dangerous human being. I began to live in a fantasy world. I saw myself doing risky, heroic things with my new rifle. In the back of my mind I became a cold blooded killer. I was going to win the war all by myself. I would become a Marine Corps legend.

When I returned to my platoon no one cared about my new occupation. Nobody was impressed with my skill as a marksman. I was told that my platoon needed a fire team leader more than they needed a sniper. So I was never set free to go hunting for VC. I stayed with the guys in my fire team…which was okay with me. And, I hate to say it, but staying with my platoon probably saved my life. The two other men who won rifles were both from Headquarters Company. One of them became a good friend. His name was Danny Martinez. A few weeks after class was over, he was shot and killed by a VC sniper. It was just before sundown. He was returning to his line. The VC sniper shot him in the chest. The third rifle winner was Sergeant Tolbert. I heard through the grapevine that he stepped on a booby trap and was badly wounded. Of the original three winners, I was the only one that was still going strong.

As time passed, I began to miss my M14. I began to regard my new sniper rifle as an inadequate weapon. It was too limited in firepower. Because it was a bolt action, I could only shoot one round at a time. Then I had to pull back the scope, and cock the bolt to load another round. It's true that the limited volume of my fire was offset by the accuracy of the weapon. But when you're shooting at an enemy who is well hidden, and you're aiming at their muzzle flash, your accuracy is uncertain. It's not like shooting at an easy to see silhouette target.

And, to make matters worse, the rifle left me feeling naked during the assault phase of a firefight. On one occasion, I had to advance with my sniper rifle on my hip shooting one bullet at a time. What a bad joke. I wanted a rifle that would put out some firepower and shake up the enemy. Fire superiority could make you feel like you were Superman. A bolt action deer rifle just wasn't up to the task. So, I decided to solve my problem by getting rid of the rifle as soon as possible. I wanted to exchange it for an M14.

My chance came sooner than I expected. While my platoon was hanging around in an LZ waiting for a ride back to our regular perimeter, a guy from another platoon began to admire the weapon. I could tell that he was dazzled by the rifle. We talked for a while.

"That's a really beautiful rifle," he said. "How accurate is it?"

"I can hit a postage stamp at two hundred meters," I said. "It's very accurate." I may have been overdoing it just a little. But I didn't care.

"Can I hold it," he asked.

"Sure," I said, un-slinging the rifle from my shoulder.

"It has a good feel," he said, raising the rifle to his shoulder, and peering through the scope. "What power is the scope?"

"It's eight power," I said. "I can easily put the cross hairs on a target the size of a human head at six hundred meters."

"Six hundred?" He said. "That's a real stretch."

I could tell the guy was entranced with the rifle, which meant that he was interested in becoming a sniper. As he played with the rifle, I could almost see his fantasy taking form. He wanted to be a dangerous human being. He wanted to be elite. If he owned the rifle it would give him bragging rights.

I'll tell you what," I said. "If you like the rifle I'll trade it to you for your M14."

"Are you serious?" He asked.

"Yeah," I said. "I'll take your M14, and you can have the sniper rifle."

"Wow!" He said, happily. "You've got a deal."

And so, I traded my sniper rifle for a run of the mill M14. I didn't care about being a sniper. In truth, I didn't want to turn into a stone cold killer. I cared more about my survival…mentally and physically. So, I went back to being an ordinary grunt serving my time in Hell. In Vietnam, if you stood out in anyway, it was dangerous because the VC would target you. And that sniper rifle was a real stand out. I was more than happy to give it up. Finally, as I've said before, I never actually saw a live VC soldier. So who was I supposed to shoot? Kids riding water buffalos? People working in the rice paddies? Old men and women? Mothers and fathers? Sons and daughters? Who was I supposed to kill? That sniper rifle was an absurd symbol of American impotence in the face of VC resistance. I mean…it was entirely useless.

You can't shoot an enemy that you can't see. The VC were shadow warriors. They fought the war on their terms. They came and went with impunity. They always got the first shot. And after they pulled our chain they would disappear like steam from a cup of coffee. By returning to an M14, I felt like I was making my way back to poor, common, suffering, mediocre, humanity. I didn't want to be an elite sniper. I preferred being one of the gang. That was the only thing that made the war endurable.

Faceless

Everyone who fought the war in Vietnam, who dropped bombs, who burned villages, who caused a lot of pain and misery, had to feel guilty. I think it was always there in the back of our minds. Killing other human beings is wrong. And whatever the justification, it couldn't placate our guilt. And because we felt guilty, we lived in a world that was separate from the world of innocent people back home in the states. Those people just went about their ordinary daily lives, going to work, going to school, raising their families, talking with friends, and caring for each other. They didn't have a clue about the daily reality of combat. They had no idea what it felt like to kill other human beings. For our part, we crossed a threshold that separated us from the light hearted reality of innocence. And, as our innocence died, the world around us became a nightmare. We did things that were cruel and savage. And we rationalize our behavior by saying: I was just following orders. Or: if I didn't kill them, they would have killed me.

And it was true. But it didn't matter. In spite of the rationale, because we had a conscience, we still felt guilty. We knew, at some deep fundamental level, that what we were doing was wrong. And yet...we did it anyway. We followed orders. If we had refused our orders we would have been Court Marshaled. But, by fighting the war, we destroyed our innocence one day at a time, one burning village at a time, one death at a time. This was the price we paid. As the war went on, we passed from sunlight into the darkness of violence. We deliberately immersed ourselves in death and destruction. That was our job…pure and simple. Red blood flowed into the green sea of the endless rice paddies. And as it flowed, we became more and more guilty. This is what war does to the young men who fight it. It cripples them with guilt.

We knew that we were killing human beings who, in the abstract, were a lot like us. We let the word enemy erase a person's humanity. Enemy is a word that can turn a human being into a non-entity. The word changes a real man or woman into a thing without a history…without an identity. It isolates and stereotypes. It negates all of those things, both mental and physical, that make us fully human. An enemy has no history, no wife or girlfriend, no sons or daughters, no sisters or brothers, no mother or father, and no dreams or goals. An enemy is a blank slate, a non-person, a piece of meat, and nothing more. But we knew, deep inside, that we were killing fellow human beings. And behind our macho mask, enforced by military discipline, there were lots of tears that should have been free to fall. But they didn't. We didn't know how to be honest with ourselves. We were trapped. Our guilt was stuffed into the back of our minds where it was free to fester and evolve into fear, anger, and despair. In the long run, I think our repressed guilt made us sick. And under a different set of circumstances, we could have been friends with our enemies. We could have gotten drunk together. We could have shared stories, and told pokes.

During one operation two VC had been killed by an airstrike. We discovered their bodies three or four days later. They were decomposing. They were swollen from the hot tropical sun. They smelled terrible. They were covered in flies. They lay sprawled in the dirt, their faces so swollen and distorted it was impossible to tell what each man had looked like. A pack lay close to one of the bodies. We carefully opened the pack. Then we rummaged through its contents. We found lots of ammo, a plastic bag full of rice, some canned goods, a few packs of Ruby Queen cigarettes, and a small wooden box. When Steve opened the box, he discovered that it contained a collection of photographs that were tied together with a red ribbon. After he untied the ribbon, we sorted through the photographs one by one. They were ordinary pictures of a young man and woman. They were holding hands and standing next to each other. There were other photos that were portraits. The man and woman were smiling and laughing. They must have been a married couple because there were also some photos of two small children. Altogether there were about fifteen photos, both black and white, and color. When we were through looking we didn't know what to do with the photos. In the end, we tied the red ribbon back around the photos, put them back inside the box, and then put the box back inside the pack. Then we walked away.

Having looked at the photos I began to feel sorry for the dead VC that owned the pack. I felt sorry for his wife and children. His collection of photos revealed some of his history. No doubt he was in love with his wife and children.

"I don't think we should have looked at those photos," Steve said.

"How could we not look?" I asked, "It was unavoidable. We just had to look. We had to know."

"I don't want to know about our fucking enemy," he said. "The less we know the better. Don't turn them into human beings."

"Our enemy has a face that isn't that different from our own face," I said. "That's what his photos revealed."

"To stay sane I can only kill faceless targets," he said. "I'm a faceless target to them. And they're a faceless target to me. That's war. Everybody loses their face."

"I'm going to think about that guy's photos for a long time to come," I said. "And maybe you're right. Maybe it was a mistake to look."

"We're animals," Steve said. "We live like animals. We think like animals. And we act like animals. Those photos belong to the civilized world. And the civilized world doesn't exist as far as we are concerned. It's only a dream."

"Maybe the dream gives us something to fight for," I said. "Maybe it will keep us alive." I was trying to sound hopeful.

"The dream didn't help that dead VC," he said.

"I wonder if his wife and kids are in the north, or the south?" I said.

"I don't care where they are," he replied. "It doesn't matter."

Steve was in denial. He just couldn't take off his macho mask. He had to go on being a tough guy. His human face beneath the mask was vulnerable. He didn't want to suffer. He didn't want to feel guilty. In fact, I think we were all in denial. We were emotionally numb. We refused to see our enemies as human beings. We had no positive feelings about them. And we had to see them as faceless targets. Otherwise, we wouldn't be able to kill them.

The Trumpet Player

Every Marine is a rifleman. The Corps is founded on this simple truth. It doesn't matter if a Marine is a cook, an engineer, a truck driver, a typist, or they are working in supply. They are, first of all, a rifleman. And this means that everyone is potentially a grunt. It means that anyone can be sent to an infantry platoon, and they will have some basic idea about what they should do. Essentially, they will be expected to shoot at the enemy. This is true even for the women who are Marines. Everyone, without exception, is a rifleman. And that also includes trumpet players.

It was another hot, sweaty day. We were sitting on our butts resting after another long tedious night on watch. There was nothing going on. I was enjoying my favorite past-time. I was drinking a cup of C-ration coffee and smoking a cigarette. We were back inside our permanent defense perimeter. It was located about five hundred meters from a large village complex off to the south. A few days earlier we had returned from another search and destroy operation that had gone on for four miserable days without contact. Personally, I was more than happy about avoiding the enemy. My nerves were on edge all of the time. I was jumpy. Any loud explosive noise would cause me to hit the deck immediately.

The airbase at Danang was about ten miles north of us. There was a rough dirt road that led off in that direction. As I sat quietly, and puffed on my cigarette, I noticed a truck slowly coming down the road. This was unusual. We didn't get many visitors by truck. Our main method of supply was by chopper. And the choppers were far and few between. I think it would be fair to say that the Marine Corps had forgotten all about us. My platoon was on its own. And this had been true for several months. We had no hot chow, no showers, we had to ration our water, and our uniforms were falling apart from dirt, mud, and sweat. Most of us avoided shaving more than once or twice a week. But we didn't give up brushing our teeth, or splashing a little water on our face in the early morning.

Anyway, the truck pulled inside of our perimeter and stopped. Then a group of ten men jumped out of its bed. I was overcome with curiosity. I didn't know what was going on. Who were these men? And why did they look so clean and fresh? They were wearing new web gear. They had new jungle boots. They had new M14s. And they were wearing new jungle utilities. I couldn't believe it. They were obviously not in the infantry. That much I could tell. They looked like kids. They were wide-eyed and very nervous. I could also see that they were completely lost, and totally out of place. The guys in my platoon, by comparison, looked like a motley bunch of ragged bums.

The mystery was soon resolved when our platoon sergeant told us that these guys were in the Marine Corps Band. They were stationed at the airbase. This meant that they were rear echelon motherfuckers. And because the Marines wanted everyone to be a rifleman, they had been assigned to our unit for a single night. The Marine Corps wanted to familiarize these musicians with life in the grunts. I thought someone was playing a joke on us. These guys were staying with us for one fucking night? And that would be enough to familiarize them with life in the grunts?

My squad was assigned three of the new guys, one for each fire team. I ended up with a guy named John, who introduced himself as a trumpet player. A trumpet player? This was totally crazy. But he seemed like a decent guy. And he had a lot of questions.

"How long have you guys been out here?" He asked, looking around. "Staying on the airbase we don't have a chance to see any guys who are in the infantry."

"Too long," I said dryly, deflecting his question.

"We've been out so long we're becoming part of the landscape," Steve said. "We're slowly turning into dirt, and mud. We are the forgotten platoon."

"Have you been attacked by the VC," he asked. "How safe is this perimeter?"

"Are you worried?" I asked.

"A little," he said. "This is Vietnam after all. There's a war going on."

"No shit," Steve said. "I thought you'd never notice."

"We get sniper fire once in a while from that far off village," I said. "But otherwise there's not much going on. You're fairly safe. The snipers are too far away to be accurate."

As we talked I found myself thinking things over. I knew he was anxious and uncomfortable. That was entirely predictable. The chance that he would be trigger-happy at night, on watch, was also predictable. So I decided to take his weapon away from him.

"Let me have your M14," I said. "I think unloading your rifle is the safest thing we can do. You won't have to stand watch tonight. You can get your beauty sleep. And I don't want you touching your rifle without my permission. Is that understood?"

I didn't wait for him to say yes. I just took his rifle, and unloaded the magazine. Then I leaned his shiny new rifle against the sandbag wall of a nearby bunker. The last thing I needed was a trigger-happy new guy standing watch. I was trying to prevent another accidental shooting. I didn't want to take any chances.

"That sure makes things easy," he said.

"You're like a tourist," I said. "You're here to look around, eat some lousy food, and talk with the guys in our platoon. Then you're gone. Tomorrow you'll be back on the airbase playing your trumpet. And we won't be anything but a vague memory."

"That's true," he said. "And I don't mind you taking my rifle away. I understand. In fact, I really don't feel comfortable carrying a weapon. I'm a musician. I carry a trumpet."

"And we are grunts," I said, "and we know what we are doing. And we don't need your help. So make yourself as comfortable as possible, and enjoy your adventure. Would you like a cup of C-ration coffee?"

"Thanks," he said, "but I think I'll pass. That stuff tastes like shit."

The rest of the day was easy going. Nothing important happened. The sun came up, and the sun went down. As usual, we set the watch, and another long night was at hand. Steve took the first four hour shift. John, the trumpet player, and I, turned in. I chose to sleep on the ground outside our bunker. I rolled up in my poncho, took off my helmet to use as a pillow, and fell asleep. John decided it would be safer to sleep inside of our bunker. I thought we were just passing through another boring night. But I was wrong. I woke up when I heard Steve shouting.

"Incoming!" He yelled. "They're shooting mortars at us! Wake up!"

He had heard the hollow thump of a mortar being fired somewhere in the far off village. The mortar shell was on its way. About five seconds later the shell exploded to our rear about fifty feet away. My adrenalin was going wild. I dove into the bunker with Steve right behind me. John was already wide awake.

"Jesus Christ!" He exclaimed loudly. "I thought you said this place was safe."

Before I could answer, another shell came down and exploded. This time it was somewhere on the west side of our perimeter, near an Amtrack that was assigned to our platoon. Everyone was rattled. Everyone was taking shelter. Nobody wanted to be hit. Nobody wanted to die.

"I think I said fairly safe," I finally replied.

"So what do we do now?" John asked. He was curled up in the fetal position, and he was on the verge of panic.

"Just hang on," I said, "and hope the motherfuckers run out of shells."

"That's it?" John said. "So we're just supposed to sit here and do nothing?"

This is the first time they've fired mortars at us," Steve said. "There's not a lot we can do."

Suddenly, as I lay inside the bunker, I heard the distant sound of an artillery barrage. Our forward observer had called for support. The night turned into day as artillery illumination lit up the landscape. I was amazed that the artillery happened so fast. Then another mortar round exploded. This time it sounded like it was in front of our lines. I soon realized that Charlie was wasting his ammunition. His mortar fire was inaccurate. It was all over the place. Still, there was a chance that Charlie would get lucky. The artillery fire continued to rain in. I heard one explosion after another coming from the village. Then some guy on the Amtrack opened fire with a .50 caliber machine gun. He was praying and spraying. He had no chance of hitting the VC who were shooting the mortars, but it didn't matter. I think the guy just felt like he had to do something. So he opened fire. Then another mortar round exploded. This time it sounded like it was near our CP. Ten seconds later I heard someone yell for the Corpsman.

"Somebody's been hit," Steve said.

"Jesus," I said quietly. "I hope they don't die."

"I can't believe this is happening to me!" John said. "Things weren't supposed to turn out like this. This is dangerous as hell. I need to get out of here. This is crazy!"

"Take it easy," I said. "Getting excited won't do anything. It'll just make everything worse."

And then the mortar fire came to a sudden end. Maybe our artillery fire scared them off. Who knows? In the aftermath, we slowly, cautiously, emerged from our bunker. I heard guys calling out names to find out if everyone was okay. As it turned out, the round that went off near our CP took out two guys, including our radioman. They were hit by shrapnel.

"Jesus Christ," John mumbled, "what have I got myself into. I don't belong here. I'm a musician. I play music. I hate guns and weapons. I don't want to kill anyone, or to be killed."

"Take it easy," I said again. "It's over, and we're still sucking air. Doesn't it feel nice to be alive?"

"You guys are crazy as hell," John said. "How do you put up with this shit from one day to the next?"

"We don't have any choice," Steve said. "We're trapped. And there's only two ways out. Either we survive our tour of duty and go home…or we die. Our fate is very simple."

And it was true. War simplifies life. It turns everything into black or white. Either you live. Or you die. What happens to you is all about good luck versus bad. You are a prisoner of random, unpredictable events.

In the morning, a medevac chopper picked up our wounded Marines. They were still alive when the chopper flew them out. Before the truck showed up to take the band members away, Steve, Jason, and I decided to ask John to make a necessary sacrifice. Essentially, we wanted him to trade all of his shiny new gear with us. I wanted his rifle and magazines. Jason wanted his web gear, his pack, and his flak jacket. Steve wanted his jungle boots, and his new utilities.

"Why not?" John said. "I'll be glad to help you guys out. When I get back to the airbase I can always order some new gear. You guys don't have that option."

And so, we traded. When we were through John looked like an unkempt bum. He looked like he was one of us. He looked like a real combat Marine. The rest of the guys in our platoon also swapped their worn out gear with the guys in the band. When they were finished the band members had an entirely different look. I was sure their commanding officer was going to be pissed off. He sent them out to our lines so they could pretend to be grunts. I don't think he imagined that they would return looking so ragged and shabby. By late morning their truck arrived to take them back to the airbase.

"It's been memorable," John said, as he walked toward the truck. "In fact, it's been a horrible experience. I feel sorry for you guys."

"We feel sorry for us too," Steve said. "But there's nothing we can do to change the game. The war just goes on, and on."

"Take care of your selves," he said. "And don't let Charlie get the upper hand."

"Charlie always has the upper hand," I said. "It's his country. He owns the place. And we belong to another army that is just passing through."

The Parking Meter

My mosquito and leech bites had become infected. When I scratched the bites it produced a small open sore. Over time this sore turned into a circular scab the size of a silver quarter. We called these sores jungle rot. My arms and legs, below the knees, were covered by them. The infection became so bad that I finally went to our platoon corpsman. I showed him the sores. Then I asked to be sent to the battalion aid station for treatment. He agreed. He said that there was nothing he could do out in the field. He told me I would need to take penicillin. And the sores would need to be washed out several times a day with peroxide. They looked terrible. They were painless, but they still bothered me. When I first came to Vietnam I'd seen villagers with these sores and I thought they were disgusting. I never thought I'd get them. But I was wrong. Living in the boonies was a disaster for our personal hygiene. We never took a shower. We were filthy with sweat and dirt. And, no doubt, these rotten conditions were largely responsible for the infection.

I caught the next supply chopper for a ride back to our battalion area. When I arrived I went straight to a large tent that served as our field hospital. Then I talked with a corpsman that was on duty. When I showed him the sores he was impressed. He told me he'd never seen a case so bad. He immediately pulled a razor out of a cabinet, lathered up my arms and legs, and shaved all the hair off. Then he produced a bottle of peroxide and proceeded to wash all of my sores. They erupted in white foam. When he was through, he cut my utility trousers off at the knees, so he could wrap my arms and legs in white bandages. Finally, he talked with a doctor for a few minutes before he gave me a shot of penicillin. My feet were also infected so I had to wear a pair of flip flops. I looked like hell. But I didn't feel all that bad.

In truth, I actually felt like I was on a vacation from my platoon perimeter out in the sticks. I felt safe for the first time in weeks. There was no enemy small arms fire to watch out for. My nerves had gone to hell over the last month or so. My reflexes, conditioned by one firefight too many, could put me on the ground in an instant. I hated sudden, loud noises. I was easily startled. Adrenalin would race through my bloodstream, my heart would pound, and sheer terror would set my mind on fire. I was fully prepared to kill someone. I was actually falling apart, but I wouldn't admit it to anyone…even myself. All of my nervous reflexes were necessary to survive combat. Coming back to the battalion area, where not much was happening, gave me a feeling of relief.

Even though my arms and legs were wrapped in bandages, I was still expected to stand watch on the battalion perimeter. As evening approached, I was told to pick up an M60 machine gun at the armory. Then I was taken to a sandbagged bunker. This was my new home for the night. Shortly after I entered the bunker, a strange looking guy from Headquarters Company joined me. His platoon commander told him to enter the bunker and stay put. The guy wore thick glasses, he was tall and gangly, and he gave me the impression that he was lost. He just didn't look or act like a Marine was supposed to look and act. The men in Headquarters Company were not grunts. They were in one kind of support unit or another. They might be on a mortar crew, they might be attached to a 106mm recoilless rifle, or they could be in supply. They didn't go out on patrol. They didn't sit in ambushes all night. And they didn't go on search and destroy operations with us. The whole point of Headquarters Company was to provide support to the four infantry companies that made up a battalion. This guy's name was Robert Jackson. I could sense that he was nervous. That's always a bad sign. I was sure he was a new guy. As I set up the machinegun, he began to talk.

"What unit are you in?" He wanted to know.

"I'm in Delta Company, first platoon."

"Why are you all bandaged up?"

"Jungle rot."

"I thought you may have been hit by shrapnel."

"No. It's just jungle rot."

Then our conversation took a sudden bizarre turn. Maybe he was trying to impress me. His imagination was impressive.

"I have three purple hearts," he suddenly said. "They've told me that I'm going to be sent home. I'm just waiting for my papers to come through."

"You have three purple hearts?"

"I got shot twice. And I was hit by shrapnel from a hand grenade."

"Really?"

"Yeah…."

"What unit are you in?"

"I'm in a supply unit."

"Supply?"

"Yeah…. Supply. We take care of C-rations and ammo for the grunts."

I could tell that he was bullshitting me. But I didn't say anything. I just went along for the ride. He was compensating for his fear by pretending to be a fearless hero. We all did that from time to time. It was normal. Being fearless was an act that attempted to nullify our true emotional state of mind. In truth, we were scared shitless. So I just let him talk.

"A few weeks ago we got in a firefight," he said. "I killed three VC. I got lucky and shot them through the head. My platoon commander said he was putting me in for a Bronze Star."

"Congratulations," I said.

"I love killing VC," he said. "I love defending my country."

The sun was going down. When I looked out of the bunker's aperture, I could see the evening shadows reaching out their long dark arms. I thought I was safe. And then everything went straight to hell. Somebody further down our line fired their weapon. This was followed by a loud response in the form of incoming fire. Directly in front of our line, so Jackson quickly told me, was an ARVN position. I had no idea what they were doing out there. It was crazy. Their position was in our field of fire. In a matter of seconds more shots were fired on both sides. Then Jackson, the war hero, aimed his M14 out of the bunker's aperture and opened fire. Although he couldn't see the ARVN troopers, he fired in their general direction. And they began shooting back at us. Bullets hit our bunker. I yelled for Jackson to cease fire, but he ignored me. So, a moment later, I reached out and took the magazine out of his rifle.

"Stop shooting!" I yelled. I was rattled. And I was angry. "Stop trying to kill the fucking ARVN. Are you crazy?"

Then, mercifully, things quieted down. We had a radio in our bunker. Jackson's platoon commander called to find out what was going on. I told him in a nervous, shaky voice that some guys on our line had decided to shoot at the ARVN.

"Is anybody hurt," he wanted to know.

"Sir," I said, "I don't think so. I didn't hear anyone yell for the corpsman."

In the aftermath, Jackson was quiet. I guess he'd run out of stories to tell. So we sat together in the gathering dark. I was glad to let silence reign. Slowly, the adrenalin in my system burned off. But just about the time I began to feel normal, there was a brand new crisis. Jackson's squad leader came into our bunker. His face was red with anger. He was really pissed off.

"Jackson!" He yelled. "I've been looking all over for you. I'm tired of your fuckups. You should have told me where you were going."

Before Jackson could say anything in his defense, his squad leader hit him in the face and knocked his glasses off. Then he hit him again, and again, and bloodied his nose and knocked him down.

"You stupid motherfucker!" He yelled. "From now on you better tell me where you're going. I'm sick of chasing you around!"

Jackson stood up and wiped the blood off his nose. Then he picked up his glasses and put them back on. Luckily, they hadn't been broken during the assault. I was embarrassed. Maybe Jackson wasn't as big a hero as he claimed? Maybe he was the platoon shit bird? I felt sorry for him. In the quiet aftermath I told his squad leader that their platoon commander had told Jackson "to stay put."

His squad leader didn't say anything. He didn't apologize. He just turned around and left the bunker.

"Your squad leader is a really nice guy," I said. I was being sarcastic.

"I'd like to kill that motherfucker," Jackson said. "I'd like to shoot him in the head."

I had no problem at all understanding his anger. If I'd been in his place, I would have felt the same way. His squad leader was a bully. I hate to say it, but the Marine Corps favors men who are bullies. These guys often get promoted because they are big, strong, and aggressive. They become squad leaders and platoon sergeants. It's just business as usual. Might makes right…that's very often the way it works in the Corps.

The rest of the night was peaceful. In the morning I had to take the M60 machine gun back to the armory and turn it in. Along the way I spotted a civilian walking beside my battalion commander. The civilian was unusual because he was carrying a golf club. As they walked along together, the man with the golf club was casually swinging it at various weeds and sprouts. The two of them were just walking and talking. I slowed down. I didn't want to cross their path. Unfortunately, my battalion commander spotted me before I could escape.

"Hey Marine," he said. "Please come over here. We'd like to talk with you."

I immediately began to panic. I had no desire to talk with my battalion commander…or an out of place guy with a fucking golf club. But orders were orders. I couldn't refuse. So I walked over to them. Then I put the M60 at order arms, and I stood at attention. My eyes were straight ahead, and my back was ramrod straight. My battalion commander walked up to me. He was smiling.

"This man is Jim Mason," he said, referring to the golfer. "He just won the US Open, and he'd like to say something to you."

"Yes sir," I said stiffly.

I had no idea what was going on. I was mildly confused. Why were they interested in talking with me? Later on, I realized they must have thought I was some sort of brave, courageous Marine. They could see that I'd been manning a machinegun, even though I was all bandaged up. I guess they thought that I'd been wounded. But it wasn't true. I was being treated for jungle rot. Anyway, the golfer walked up to me.

"I'd like to tell you how proud all of us Americans are over the job you Marines are doing," he said. "You're fighting the communists, and you're winning the war. It has to be terribly difficult. But it's something that needs to be done. We have to stop the spread of world-wide communism. And I just want to tell you that you have the support of the entire nation. And we wish you well."

"Thank you sir," I said.

Then my battalion commander dismissed me. So I did an about face, hoisted the machinegun to port arms, and then I marched off toward the armory like a proper Marine.

The golfer didn't talk with me. He talked at me. He could have been a mad man speaking to a parking meter. If I'd had the chance to speak my mind, I would have told him he was full of shit. The golfer didn't have a clue about what was really going on. He was visiting the battalion area to inspire the troops with political propaganda, which was totally out of touch with reality. I knew we were not winning the war. We were losing because we could not defeat the North Vietnamese. We were only fighting to prevent the south from losing. We were fighting to preserve the status quo...which was a stalemate. And you can't win a war by staying on the defense. And that's all we were doing. We were defending South Vietnam. And I knew, in the end, the north would prevail. It was inevitable. Vietnam would be reunited. The VC had a just cause, and they were willing to pay the price. And eventually, the United States military would experience the same forlorn destiny as the French and Japanese. We would lose. I was sure of that. In fact, I often thought that we were fighting on the wrong side. The VC were far more courageous, and far more dedicated to their cause than the ARVN troops. After the French lost their war, our politicians should have supported Ho Chi Minh, and reunification. Instead, paranoia took over, and now millions of people were in the process of dying for a lost cause.

More, More, More….

One day I was sitting in the battalion aid station waiting for my shot of penicillin when a close friend from my platoon was brought in. His name was Jack Hanson. He was one of our platoon squad leaders. On a sweep through a nearby village, a guy named Pete Nottingham had touched off a booby trap. It mangled one of his legs. Corporal Hanson had been hit in the back by a chunk of shrapnel. It tore out a chunk of his flesh. The wound wasn't serious enough for him to be evacuated to the division hospital at Chu Lai. Luckily, the shrapnel didn't penetrate his rib cage. I sat and watched as they stitched a small drain pipe into the wound.

"So now you've earned a Purple Heart," I said. I was trying to be cheerful.

"Yeah," he said with no enthusiasm. "It's just what I fucking need."

"How's everyone in the platoon doing?" I asked.

"We're surviving," he said.

His spirits were low. I could tell he was worried.

"That new village is a bitch," he said. "I'm afraid we're going to lose more people to booby traps."

"Maybe you should take a break," I said. "Take some light duty until you feel better."

"I can't do that," he said. "There's too much to do. We're already short of men."

He made me feel guilty. I was taking it easy in the battalion area with my case of jungle rot while he, and the other guys in my platoon, were putting their lives on the line. I felt like a slacker.

"How are Steve and Jason doing," I asked.

"Good…as far as far as I know," he said. "I don't see them that often. They're in a different section of the perimeter."

I had the feeling that he didn't want to talk a lot. I think he was still feeling slightly rattled. He was trying hard to put on a brave face. He was struggling to regain his composure before he returned to our line. I had a bad feeling about that. But then, I had a bad feeling about almost everything in Vietnam. It was a country where feeling bad was normal. If you felt good, you were out of touch with reality and probably insane.

"I don't think you should go back," I said. "I think you should take a day or two off. Let your body heal up. What's the fucking hurry? The war isn't going away."

"I can't do it," he said. "I just can't do it. I have a squad to lead."

A few minutes later the corpsman finished working on him. Then Corporal Hanson left the tent. He didn't say goodbye. He just left. He was in a hurry to get back to our platoon perimeter. And that was the last time I ever saw him. Two days later he was dead. During a squad patrol he touched off another booby trap. It blew him apart. It turned him into a bloody chunk of meat. And it seriously wounded two other men. One of them was a close friend of mine named Ralph Anderson. Everyone called him Andy. We were writing letters to a couple of young women who knew each other. Once Andy was placed in a VA hospital in the states, the girl he was writing to drove all the way from San Francisco, to Huston, to stay with him. The girl I was writing to kept me informed. The news wasn't that good. Andy was in bad shape. But eventually, he would recover. The war was heating up. The VC were planting more and more booby traps and anti-personnel mines. Their units were more active. There were more and more fire fights. They were becoming more aggressive. And we were taking more and more casualties. More, more, more…. As we Americans built up our ground forces, Charlie reciprocated with greater numbers of his own. Then too, we were pushing into his territory south of the airbase at Danang.

There was a muddy river that we crossed over one day. We walked across a bridge that had been partially blown up. It still had some steel beams that we could hang onto and use for footing. I was told that the southern side of the river was Indian Territory that belonged to Charlie. I don't know the name of the river. It doesn't matter. After we crossed the river we never went back to the airbase. We just moved farther and farther south.

And we had lots of company. There were other units from our battalion that were set up a few miles away. At night, occasionally, one of our neighbor's positions would suddenly erupt in gunfire. Red tracers would streak off into the night sky. Either they were being probed, or somebody was trigger happy. These were violent, dream like episodes of madness. Men were trying to kill each other in the middle of the night. These defensive positions were like small islands in a green sea. I would hunker down in my foxhole and watch, waiting for the sun to rise, waiting for the new day to arrive. And each day was like a stepping stone on the path to my deliverance…my flight home. And as my time in the country grew short, I became more and more nervous over being killed or badly wounded. My fears were well grounded. The war was heating up.

After a week or so, my jungle rot was under control, and I was able to rejoin my platoon. I was surprised at how many new guys there were. I actually felt like a stranger. Fortunately, Steve and Jason were still in my squad so I didn't feel completely alone. The new guys needed to be closely watched until they adjusted to combat. This was especially true when we went out on patrol, or to conduct a search and destroy operation. During one such action Jason was walking along behind a new guy who was part of an M60 crew attached to my squad. We were moving down a narrow path toward another small village. The path went through a tree line. The guy with the machine gun was about twenty or so feet in front of Jason when he stepped on a booby-trapped Howitzer round that was buried in the dirt. There was a hell of an explosion! When the dust cleared I could see that the guy with the machine gun had been blown off the path and into the weeds. He was in really bad shape. His body and machine gun were twisted and broken. He had no arms or legs. There was nothing the corpsman could do. Luckily, the guy was unconscious so he felt no pain. He bled out in two or three minutes. Jason had been knocked silly by the concussion of the explosion. He had blood coming out of his nose and ears. He couldn't hear anything. He was having trouble speaking. And when he tried to stand up he lost his balance and fell back down. Luckily, he hadn't been hit by shrapnel. The same was not true for the new guy who had been just ahead of the machine gunner. He took a hit in his right leg. In one horrible moment we lost three men, including my close friend Jason. We called in for a medevac. I helped to put Jason on the chopper. I said goodbye. I don't think he heard me. He was conscious but disoriented. Then we burned the village to the ground. There were no civilians present. The village was deserted. It was just another death trap. It felt good to see it go up in flames.

Steve and I were depressed about losing Jason. We were angry. But there was nothing we could do to change the nature of the game. We were losing men one and two at a time with no shots being fired. Charlie had us by the balls. He didn't have to shoot at us. He could be miles away when his booby-traps went off. What we needed was a change in tactics that put the VC on the defense. But that never happened. We just made the same mistakes over and over, as if losing men was unimportant, as if we were brainless cannon fodder. And, in truth, I think we actually were. We were walking targets. That was our job. We went out on patrol, or some bigger operation, and we walked around until we drew VC small arms fire. Then we called in artillery, Huey gunships, or an airstrike. It was a simple set of tactics that were designed to get us killed. The VC were far more inventive. They used the land and the people against us. And, basically, there was nothing we could do to defeat them once and for all. We were a small drop of oil in a vast sea of muddy water. We didn't mix.

Victory?

When I jumped off the chopper I spotted four bodies lying off to one side of the LZ. They were wrapped in ponchos. The sky was overcast. It was drizzling rain. The wind from the chopper's rotors rustled and toyed with the ponchos. I was afraid the ponchos would blow off and reveal the dead bodies. I didn't want to see the dead bodies. The sight of the dead would only worsen my fear of death. Their muddy boots were sticking out so I knew they were Marines. I felt sorry for them. But at the same time, I knew they were at peace. My greatest sorrow was for their mothers and fathers, their sisters and brothers, and their friends. I knew their deaths would leave a deep ache in the hearts of all those who loved them. After the men in my squad were on the ground, a group of guys in the LZ carried the dead Marines to the empty chopper and placed them aboard. The task took less than five minutes. I later found out that the Marines were killed when their platoon was ambushed not too far from the LZ. We assumed that Charlie was still in the area. And, not long after we arrived, we set out to find him. We were looking for a fight.

We formed a column and then headed down a path toward a large rice paddy and a distant village. After we reached the rice paddy we spread out and formed a skirmish line. Then we kneeled down and waited for the order to move forward. I think everyone knew there was a good chance that we would get hit as we closed the distance to the village. We were doing our job. We were deliberately making targets out of ourselves. The village was about four hundred meters away. Our platoon sergeant finally yelled for us to move out. We stood up. Then we entered the rice paddy and began to wade through it. Warm water squished into my boots. I could feel the muddy bottom. It was slippery. I knew Charlie would wait until we were too far into the rice paddy to withdraw when they opened fire. I knew they were afraid of being hit by artillery…or an airstrike. I knew they would wait until we were so close we couldn't use supporting fire without hitting our own men. It was a tactic they called 'grabbing us by the belt buckle.' Contact at close range also gave them better targets to shoot at. We moved forward. We were waiting for the first shot. We didn't know how many VC were in the village. I listened for the sound of people doing ordinary things. I listened for the sound of dogs barking and children playing. All I heard was the sound of my own feet moving through shin deep water. I thought about the dead Marines back in the LZ. It was so easy to die in Vietnam. And I was so afraid of dying. Nevertheless, I moved forward with the rest of the guys in my platoon. I had no choice. I was a prisoner of circumstance.

The instant we heard the first volley of VC fire everyone splashed down on their belly and squirmed up against the nearest rice paddy dike for cover. Then we raised our heads, aimed our rifles, and returned fire. Bullets snapped by just several feet over our heads. They made a loud snap like firecrackers. As they zipped into the rice paddy water, geysers shot up. They hit the dikes we were hiding behind with a dull thud. When the shooting started we were about one hundred meters from the tree line that defined the edge of the village. The tree line twinkled with a series of muzzle flashes. Several minutes after we began to return fire, the order was given to move forward. Three or four guys in one fire team would jump up and race to the next dike. Then, after they splashed back down, they would begin firing to cover the forward advance of the other fire teams in their squad. This movement is known as fire and maneuver. It insures that any fire team moving forward is covered by other fire teams. The whole point is to maintain fire superiority.

I'm not sure how much time passed during the fight. Time always seemed to slow down once the shooting started. Maybe this effect is related to the flood of adrenalin you experience? I don't know.... I do know that once I concentrated on the target, I would stop thinking about death and being afraid. In fact, I would stop thinking at all. My mind would clear itself of thoughts as I became an intimate part of my weapon. During firefights I was always totally focused. I was reacting by instinct. So much of our fear in this world is related to our thoughtful expectations of the future. And, in Vietnam, our future expectations were always bad. That's the nature of war. The future becomes hopelessly grim. We're not sure that tomorrow is even going to arrive. Fear often left me feeling helpless. But once I began to fight back the fear disappeared. Killing the enemy was very therapeutic. And, if we succeeded, it gave us a strong feeling of liberation that verged on elation. Victory over a deadly enemy is better than drugs. It can turn being alive into a miracle.

Then I heard several men yell for the platoon corpsman. Men had been hit. Men were down, but our line never slowed. We continued to rush forward. The twinkling of muzzle flashes seemed to be decreasing. Either the VC were pulling out, or they were being killed and wounded. When we were about twenty meters from the tree line the order was given to stand up and charge. We put on our war face. We screamed and hollered. We growled like wild animals. A few more guys yelled for the corpsman. We kept moving forward. As we got closer to the tree line, I saw fewer and fewer muzzle flashes, until they disappeared. Charlie called it quits. Once again he pulled his shadowy vanishing act. When we entered the tree line we found two wounded VC, and three who were dead. Someone immediately shot the wounded VC. We had no mercy. We never took wounded prisoners.

The village was deserted. We automatically began to set it on fire. No order was needed. Men just broke out their cigarette lighters and torched the thatch roofs of the houses. My squad leader, Sergeant Morris Adams was yelling for us to watch out for booby-traps.

"Be careful," he said. "Stay off the fucking paths. Walk in the weeds. Walk through the gardens. Hack your way through the hedges. Keep your eyes open. Watch out for trip wires. Watch out where you put your fucking feet."

A few minutes later I saw two Huey gunships fly by overhead. They were looking for the disappearing VC. As I watched, they circled back around, and seemed to be lining up on a target. Then, the chopper in the lead dipped its nose and fired a salvo of rockets. What it was shooting at was out beyond the edge of the village. I was sure it was hitting the VC that had been shooting at us. Seen from the air, the VC had suddenly become vulnerable. They couldn't run and hide from the gunships.

"I hope they kill every last one of those motherfuckers," Steve said angrily. "I want to count their dead, broken bodies one by one. It will be good for my morale."

The gunships made pass after pass. They used up all of their ammo, and then they flew away. After we moved through the village we discovered a tree line that snaked its way toward another village about five hundred meters away. There was a spot in that tree line that was still smoking from the rockets fired by the gunships. If we ventured out to that spot I was sure we'd find a lot of dead VC. Steve was curious. He wanted to go and take a look. So I volunteered my fire team, and the three of us trudged down a path that ran through the tree line. To be safe, we walked in the weeds to one side of the path. About three hundred meters down the path we discovered twelve VC bodies. They were in terrible shape. Some were missing arms and legs, and some had their bellies blown open. They were riddled with bullets. A few were floating face down in the nearby rice paddy. The rest were sprawled all over the path. I thought there'd be a few wounded among their number. But I was wrong. They were all dead. The gunships had been very thorough. They did a masterful job.

Another squad joined us. We collected the enemy rifles, hand grenades, and anything else that could be used as a weapon. Then we returned to our platoon position. As things turned out, we had two dead and three wounded of our own. That meant that our ratio for the day was seventeen to two. Those numbers were high enough to qualify as a real victory. But the numbers left me feeling hollow and empty inside. They didn't mean anything. The quantitative numbers were only an impersonal measure that dehumanized the tragedy of men fighting and dying. On the other hand, the qualitative reality of death on the battlefield couldn't be measured by a simple ratio. You couldn't put a number to grief and sorrow. You couldn't put a number to anger and hatred. You couldn't put a number to fear and terror. These feelings were real. They were an essential part of the war. And we could always trust our feelings. They never let us down.

This was the last firefight I was in. A few days after we returned to our regular platoon position, I was told to get my shit ready because I was going home. This good news came as a surprise. My company had trained for a month or so, on Okinawa, before we were ordered into Vietnam. The time we spent training, I found out, was included in the length of my stay in Vietnam. This meant that I was getting out earlier than I planned. I felt very relieved. I was definitely ready to leave the country. The war was heating up. More and more new troops were arriving. And the VC were becoming more and more aggressive. I actually felt sorry for the new guys in my platoon. Unlike me, and my friends, they had no time to adjust to the country or combat operations. They were confronted with the threat of violence from the moment they arrived. The guys in my original platoon had been slowly introduced. In retrospect, we had it very, very easy. But those days were long gone. The war was getting big and ugly.

Welcome Home

My mind was like a bottle filled with a liquid called courage. When I first entered Vietnam the bottle was full. I enjoyed taking risks. I felt like I was immortal. I volunteered for jobs that put my life on the line. I wanted to win the war. I wanted to be brave. I wanted to defeat Charlie. I believed that the war needed to be fought. But I was young and naïve. It would take some time for the violence of the war to scrub away the thin veneer that concealed my fear of death. Over time, the war slowly wore me down. I lost my sense of purpose and meaning. The world no longer made any sense. My existence made no sense. Why had I survived while so many of my friends had died? Their deaths were a bad surprise. Bang! They were suddenly dead. And there was nothing that could be done to bring them back. I don't think that bad luck can be explained in rational terms. It just happens…or not. And because we can't explain it, we can never come to terms with it. And the deaths of my friends left me feeling guilty. Why them and not me?

By the time I climbed aboard the airplane for my flight out of the country the bottle was empty. I had no courage left. I was a nervous wreck. Loud sounds drove me crazy. I hated taking orders. My hands shook from time to time. I was hyper vigilant. I couldn't relax. I wanted to fist fight with some big guy and kick his ass. I was angry. I felt like I'd been played for a chump. I no longer believed in the war. I no longer believed in humanity. I wanted to forget that I'd ever been in

Vietnam. I wanted to stop the incessant flow of my war memories. I wanted to regain my innocence. I wanted to be happy again. I wanted to fall in love. But there was no air left in the tire. I was twenty years old, and I felt like I was going on ninety.

As I sat on the airplane waiting for it to taxi out to the runway for take-off, I glanced out of a small window next to my seat. I saw a crowd of rear echelon motherfuckers. They were dressed in new uniforms. And they were following a woman who had bright red hair. The sight made me curious. Who was the woman? And why were so many men following her around? The guy sitting next to me told me the woman was Ann Margaret, the Hollywood actress. She, like a number of other celebrities, had decided to pay a visit to the troops to boost their morale. I wasn't impressed. The troops these celebrities visited were in the rear. They didn't need to have their morale boosted. These guys weren't even in the war. They stayed on the airbase, lived in nice Quonset huts with air conditioning, had access to showers and hot food, and never fired a shot in anger. The troops that needed to have their morale boosted were out in the boonies. They were covered in mud, dirt, and sweat. They wore old uniforms and boots, and they were eating C-rations three times a day. Taking a shower was a nice fantasy. In fact, for every Marine out in the field fighting the war, there were six rear echelon motherfuckers providing support. I was jealous. I was still covered in dry rice paddy mud. I stank from body order. I smelled like Vietnam but I didn't care. I was leaving Vietnam behind and that was all that mattered. I was still alive and in one piece. I had survived. In spite of being strung out, I felt happy and guilty at the same time. I was happy to be out of the war. But I felt guilty about leaving the guys in my platoon. When I left, I said goodbye to everyone. Then I climbed onto a supply chopper for a flight back to my battalion area where I turned in my rifle at the armory. An hour or so later, I climbed onto a truck with a few other guys for the ride to the airbase. After I arrived, I stood in line, checked in, and then I had to wait a few hours. Eventually, I was placed on a military aircraft for a flight back to Okinawa. From Okinawa, I was going to catch another military flight that was headed to El Toro Airbase, near Santa Anna, California. I was pleased with how quickly I was processed for my flight home. There were no long delays. All the pieces clicked into place. I was moving rapidly toward freedom from the death and destruction of the war. The worst year of my life was coming to an end.

The flight to Okinawa was uneventful. As the hours passed by I began to think about Suziko. I decided to look her up if I had time. It would be nice to see her. After I arrived, I checked in at the transient barracks. The hour was late. They assigned me a bed, and they gave me two sheets and a blanket. After I took a shower and cleaned up, I made up the bed. Then I lay down and tried to sleep. But the bed was uncomfortable. I began to toss and turn. So I took the blanket and lay down on the concrete floor. I wrapped the blanket around me like a poncho. I was used to sleeping on the hard ground. In less than five minutes I was sound asleep.

It was going to take some time for me to readjust. I'd left the war…but the war hadn't left me. It was going to take some time for me to stop ducking and flinching every time I heard a sudden loud sound. It was going to take some time for me to stop searching tree lines for the shadowy silhouettes of the enemy. It was going to take some time for me to stop looking for trip wires and punji pits when I walked down the sidewalk. It was going to take some time for me to stop waiting anxiously for the VC to fire the first shot. It was going to take some time for me to stop hating politicians and other authority figures…the assholes that sent me and my bodies off to fight and die. The violence of the war had conditioned my mind and body to survive. And now that I was going home, my mind and body were all out of context. My instinctive defenses were still up. The world I was returning to was relatively peaceful, and all of my defenses were no longer necessary…but that didn't matter. I couldn't control them. They were automatic, like breathing in, and out. And my memories of the war would be like a dark thunder cloud on the sunny landscape of civil society. I retained my fear of a violent death. It wouldn't go away. I couldn't return to who I was before I went to war. I was no longer innocent. I had seen too much of the dark side of the human condition. It ruined my faith in humanity. The war had changed me forever. It turned me into a nihilistic cynic. What could I believe in? Our government was a sad joke. Our military was impotent and incompetent. Religion was a delusion. The war had poisoned and destroyed my naiveté. I knew that I was destined to be a misfit. The war in Vietnam liberated the cruelest aspects of my own psyche. Some of the things I'd done would get me a long prison sentence in civilian life. And yet, in Vietnam those things were completely normal. Fighting a war flips morality on its head. Good becomes bad. And now there were two conflicted sides to my personality. One side, as memories flowed through my mind, went on with the war. The other side would have to pretend to be a civilized human being. In other words, in order to fit in, I would have to hide the fact that I'd been to Vietnam. I would have to keep my experience a secret if I wanted to re-enter polite society. I would have to try and leave the war behind. Because war is never polite, I would have to try and bury my memories in the back of my mind. But I knew that repression was not a solution. It would only become a cause for mental turmoil. I was sure that I would have nightmares about the war, and that I would have vivid, intense memories. One way, or the other, the war would find a way to express itself. I knew the ugly truth would not go away peacefully. It was more like a red fire truck than a pair of sneakers.

After I ate morning chow, I decided to check in, and find out when my flight for the states would be leaving. I was hoping to have enough time to go and look for Suziko. After checking a roster, a sergeant told me that my flight would be leaving in two days. That was more than enough time to find Suziko. I retrieved some civilian clothes from my sea bag. Even though they were somewhat wrinkled, I put them on. Then, after I signed out, I walked out to the main road and caught a taxi for Naha. Twenty minutes later the taxi dropped me off at Suziko's apartment building. Unfortunately, when I knocked on her door no one answered. I tried knocking several more times without success. I had no idea where she was, or when she would be home. In fact, I thought she may have moved. So, I decided to visit the Blue Fox, the tavern where she worked later that day. In the meantime, I decided to do some casual shopping. I would just enjoy being on my own for the first time in a long while. It was a beautiful morning. I wouldn't have to follow anyone's orders. I could go where I wanted. It was nice to be free. The hours passed by. I ate lunch at a small restaurant, and I bought an American newspaper from a news stand. There was a nice quiet park nearby. I found a bench to sit on. Then I opened the paper and I began to read. There was an article on the troop buildup. And there was another story about the growing casualty rate. Finally, there was a report on war protests. This was all brand new information. Having been out in the boonies for so long, I had no idea what was going on. I lost touch. We didn't have access to newspapers or magazines. My platoon was in its own small world taking care of daily reality. We were disconnected from the greater world. In particular, I didn't know about the war protests. The article said that they were small, but growing, as discontent over the war spread from one college campus to another. I thought everyone in the United States supported the war. My first reaction was surprise. Then I thought that these war protestors were undermining our effort. They seemed to be self-serving traitors who were deliberately playing into the enemy's hands. It was disturbing to know that a group of young Americans were being so anti-American. Whose side were these protestors on? If they were against the war, which was being fought to defend democracy in South Vietnam, did that mean they were supporting the communists? I was confused. It seemed to me that the guys that were fighting and dying in Vietnam were being stabbed in the back by welltodo members of my own generation. I thought they were putting their own selfish interests above the needs of the country. They were supporting an enemy that was killing American and South Vietnamese troops. This was a terrible betrayal. To be sure, this article provoked a latent patriotic bias I was unaware of. I began to hate the protestors. I thought they were smug, self-righteous, moralizing cowards. But my part in the war was over and done. I was going home. I was still among the living, and that was all that mattered.

Late that afternoon, I walked into the Blue Fox. I was hoping to find Suziko working the tables. But she wasn't there. And when I asked around, nobody knew where she was. Months had passed since I'd last seen her, and the world had obviously changed. Apparently, she no longer worked at the tavern. She was gone, and I was disappointed. I often thought about her while I was seated in my fox hole late at night. I missed her. She was my one link to sanity during the course of the entire war. I bought a couple of drinks to feel better. Then I returned to the transient barracks and took a nap. Later that evening, after I ate supper, I took a long hot shower. I wanted to scrub the last of the war away. I wanted to wash it down the drain. I wanted the war to disappear forever. I wanted to emerge from the shower as a clean human being, free of my bad memories. But, of course, that was impossible.

A day later I caught my flight back to the states. It was aboard a military 707 jetliner. The flight took eleven long hours, including a stop in Hawaii to refuel. After we arrived at El Toro Airbase, we filed off the airplane, picked up our sea bags, and then made our way through customs. Then we were escorted to another transient barracks. It had been a long, and unremarkable, trip home. It was early afternoon. The sun was shining. Myself, and two other Marines, decided to dress up in our civvies, and then take a trip into town. We wanted to visit a bar and drink a few beers. I wasn't certain that I was old enough at twenty. But I decided to take a risk. A cold beer would be very nice. We walked off the base. Then we decided to hitchhike into the downtown area. In order to do that, we had to stand on the entry ramp of the local freeway. I thought we'd be picked up in a short amount of time. But no one offered us a ride. Every passerby could see that we were Marines. Our haircuts were a dead giveaway. We waited about a half hour with no luck at all. Car after car went by. Then I saw a hopped up 1956 Chevy. It turned onto the entry ramp and then accelerated. I saw four guys with long hair inside the car. As they approached, the driver swerved off the road to run us over. He forced us to scramble into the nearby weeds. And as the car flew by, someone inside threw a large cup of Coca Cola at us. Then some guy leaned out of the passenger window and screamed "baby killers!" A moment later they were gone. I had Coca Cola all over my shirt. It was sticky and uncomfortable. I was shocked and surprised. I couldn't understand why someone would do something like that. It was our first evening back in the states. The assholes in the Chevy had stereotyped us and then struck out. Less than a week earlier we had been waging a war against the VC and risking our lives. I thought we deserved some respect. But the guys in the Chevy had a different idea. They turned us into targets. They turned us into their enemy. I began to realize that our country had changed. The America I left to fight in Vietnam was not the same country I returned to. There were members of my generation that were targeting veterans with harassment. They wanted to make themselves look morally superior by turning veterans into social pariahs. They wanted to shame us into feeling guilty for our service in the war. Because they thought the war was wrong, they also thought the guys that fought it should be punished. When I came back I didn't expect a brass band or a red carpet. I just wanted to go home and heal. I wanted to find some peace. Then I wanted to get a job, find a beautiful woman, get married, raise a family, and forget about the war. I didn't expect to be attacked, harassed, or treated like a psychopath because I was a veteran. After we talked things over, we decided to go back to the airbase. There was really nothing else to do. The cold beer would have to wait for another day.

"Welcome home," one of the guys said as we trudged back toward the airbase.

"Yeah," I said. "For what it's worth…welcome home."

Note

My unit was Delta Company, 1st Battalion, 9th Marine Regiment, of the 3rd Marine Division. In 1969, after four years of combat operations, the battalion was taken out of the field. It had the highest casualty rate in Marine Corps history. Seven hundred and forty seven young Marines had died. There were only around eight hundred men in a battalion. The unit was on the perimeter at the siege of Khe Sanh. It was involved in the hill fights. And it was stationed on the deadly 'hill of angels', known as Con Thien. General Vo Nguyen Giap, the Commander of the NVA, told Ho Chi Minh, that he would utterly destroy the 1st Battalion, 9th Marines…as a birthday present. He called the battalion 'di bo chet'. This translates into the term: walking dead. But that never happened. The Marines survived. And they eventually adopted the name given to them by Giap. They became 'the walking dead'.